THE ISIS THREAT: WEIGHING THE OBAMA ADMINISTRATION'S RESPONSE

HEARING

BEFORE THE

COMMITTEE ON FOREIGN AFFAIRS
HOUSE OF REPRESENTATIVES

ONE HUNDRED THIRTEENTH CONGRESS

SECOND SESSION

SEPTEMBER 18, 2014

Serial No. 113–219

Printed for the use of the Committee on Foreign Affairs

Available via the World Wide Web: http://www.foreignaffairs.house.gov/ or
http://www.gpo.gov/fdsys/

U.S. GOVERNMENT PRINTING OFFICE

89–814PDF   WASHINGTON : 2014

COMMITTEE ON FOREIGN AFFAIRS

CONTENTS

THE ISIS THREAT: WEIGHING THE OBAMA ADMINISTRATION'S RESPONSE

THURSDAY, SEPTEMBER 18, 2014

House of Representatives,
Committee on Foreign Affairs,
Washington, DC.

The committee met, pursuant to notice, at 11:34 a.m. in room 2171, Rayburn House Office Building, Hon. Ed Royce (chairman of the committee) presiding.

Chairman ROYCE. This hearing will come to order.

This morning we welcome Secretary Kerry back to the committee to weigh the administration's response to the ISIL threat, and a threat it is.

Never has a terrorist organization occupied such a sanctuary. Never has such a terrorist organization had the access to the abundant natural resources that ISIL has at its disposal. Never has a terrorist organization possessed the heavy weaponry or the cash or the personnel that ISIL has today. And its brutality, of course, is unmatched.

This committee, on a bipartisan basis, has been pushing the administration to confront this threat. For months I pressed the administration for drone strikes, as the terrorists columns advanced on Iraqi cities. That is what the Iraqis wanted, and it is what many in our Embassy in Baghdad wanted. Ranking Member Engel has been pushing to arm the Free Syrian Army. That is what the President's entire national security team wanted, including General David Petraeus, who headed the CIA at the time and frankly, the White House hesitancy on this has put us in a situation where ISIL has gained a lot of ground.

But where we are today is we, I think agree on the steps that will turn the tables, turn the table on ISIL. Pushing Maliki to the side to give Iraqis a chance at representative government is one of the issues of Secretary of State has worked on. Aid to our allies from the air and I should say here we saw 116,000 air strikes during the opening days of the first Gulf War, when Kuwait was occupied.

We need a robust response from the air, giving the Kurdish Peshmerga and many Iraqi units the backing they need to confront ISIL and using other elements against this wretched terrorist group. Not just the Free Syrian Army, but we recall the Sunni Awakening, when they rose up against al-Qaeda, and the fact that that strategy worked against al-Qaeda, it can work against ISIL.

We have here an organization on the ground, a jihadist group that frankly has carried out massacres of Christians, Yazidis, Shia, Sunnis, beheading two American journalists, enslaving minority women, turning them into concubines, frankly, a jihadist group that demands the international community come together to suppress and defeat it.

And it is good that we have finally acknowledged that we do have a partner on the ground in Aleppo, Syria, just not one that is adequately trained and adequately supplied to take on the formidable ISIL and Hezbollah-backed regime in Damascus. But ISIL has to be attacked in Syria. It has to be attacked in Syria because the sanctuary, the base of operations, base of training is on the Syrian side of that border, and to defeat a terrorist group you have got to go after their sanctuary. And as we hit them from the air, there has to be engagement of the ISIL forces on the ground that are already attacking Aleppo. Yesterday's House vote was a first step, and we trust that you will be in close touch with the committee, Mr. Secretary, as you get this training program off the ground. So it is us in the air, it is the local Kurdish and Arab units providing the combat troops on the ground, maintaining the momentum against ISIS to defeat it.

And the administration is right to get as many others in the region and from around the world to step up. This isn't just our fight. The Secretary is just returning from a trip to the region, and has been talking with other Nations, some who will contribute cash, others intelligence or military support. But we would like to hear more about the pledges of support. Just who will be bringing what to the table? How firm is their resolve? And while we are aware of the plight of those Turkish diplomats that are being held captive, the bottom line still is that Turkey is a NATO ally, and it is not pulling its weight. And that has to change.

Of course not all in the region will play a constructive role. Qatar comes to mind. And the committee certainly doesn't see Iran's regime doing anything other than what it has done for the last 30 years, bringing destruction to the region through their machinations.

We look forward to meeting with General Allen, who you just appointed, Mr. Secretary, as the Special Envoy for the global coalition to counter ISIL, to discuss these and other issues.

The ISIL threat is a dramatic wakeup call. While some claim that the threats to the United States were receding, the reality is that a tidal wave of militancy is cresting here. Unfortunately, a lot of the recruitment occurs through the Internet.

And the good news is that the President has now acknowledged that this threat must be confronted. We must have a sustained commitment that only the Commander in Chief can marshal. This hearing will be one of many to evaluate the administration's resolve and strategy to defeat this threat.

And I will now turn to our ranking member, Mr. Elliott Engel, of New York, for his opening comments.

Mr. ENGEL. Thank you very much, Mr. Chairman.

Mr. Chairman, the decisions we now face are decisions of life and death. The course we set in the next several weeks and months will have ramifications around the world for years to come. And this situation demands that we set party politics aside.

Mr. Chairman, we are grateful, as always, for your even, bipartisan leadership, and I want to identify myself with your remarks.

Mr. Secretary, thank you for coming before us today, and thank you for your decades of tireless service to our country, for your work during uncertain and dangerous times.

Congratulations to you and the administration for asking for a vote and winning the vote in the House yesterday to aid and train Syrian rebels. But Mr. Secretary, in my view the step the House took yesterday was long overdue. Over 1½ years ago I introduced the Free Syria Act, which would have armed and trained vetted members of the opposition at that point. We can't know what would have happened if we had acted then, but we do know that since then tens of thousands of men, women, and children have lost their lives, millions have been driven from their homes, and ISIS has grown and spilled across the Iraqi border, leaving behind a trail of destruction and bloodshed.

Now that we are on the verge of training and equipping moderate Syrians, this must be considered only a first step to address a far-reaching threat. A vast stretch of land in Syria and Iraq is now in the crushing grip of ISIS. Left to fester, ISIS terrorists would rule the cradle of civilization with a brand of barbarism out of history's darkest chapters, and offer safe haven to those who share their hateful and false ideology.

Whether ISIS or al-Qaeda, Hamas or Hezbollah, terrorists thrive in ungoverned spaces and spread their lies and hatred. We have seen this before. In Afghanistan, after the Russians were driven out with American help, the Taliban planted their flag, and al-Qaeda found a safe place to plan attacks against our country, including September 11, 2001, against my city. Make no mistake, if we don't act it will happen again. So today I hope we can explore the way we move forward from here. There are a few points I think are especially important.

First, building a credible international coalition. It is critical that our partners in the region play a leading role combating ISIS. But the entire international community has a stake in this effort. Thousands of foreign fighters from dozens of countries have poured into Syria to join ISIS. And these battle-hardened extremists could launch attacks when they return home. I look forward to hearing about your progress with leaders in the Middle East and Europe in addressing the foreign fighter issue, and building an international coalition to degrade and destroy ISIS.

Secondly, how do we address all aspects of the conflict? The border between Syria and Iraq is gone. We are now dealing with a single theater. I believe Congress has a responsibility to consider a new AUMF, authorization for the use of military force, that is specifically tailored to the current situation.

Next, how do we ensure that our support of the moderate Syrian opposition isn't just limited to combating ISIS? The Assad regime continues to torture and murder its own citizens. We cannot lose sight of the fact that Assad must go. He is a magnet for extremists and foreign fighters and this crisis will not end as long as he remains in power. I believe that this train and equip program is the best chance we have to bring about a negotiated political solution in Syria. Empowering the moderate opposition is the only way to compel Assad to the negotiating table.

Make no mistake, there is no military solution to this crisis. How can we shape an environment that is conducive to bringing the parties to the table and moving toward a negotiated solution? Mr. Secretary, you know better than anybody we are out of good choices. There are no good choices in Iraq and Syria. No one in this country or this Congress wants to be dragged into another open-ended war. But I fear now, of all the bad choices, the worst choice would be to do nothing. That is why I am glad that the House did the right thing yesterday in the vote.

As the President said last week, we will hunt down terrorists who threaten our country wherever they are. We need to do this, and we need to do it right.

So I thank you again, Mr. Chairman.

And Mr. Secretary, I look forward to your testimony.

Chairman ROYCE. And, Mr. Secretary, welcome back.

All of the members here are pleased to be joined by Mr. John Kerry, 68th Secretary of State of the United States. And without objection, I will add that the witness's full prepared statement will be part of the record.

Members here will have 5 calendar days to submit any statements or questions or extraneous material that they want to put in the record.

Chairman ROYCE. Mr. Secretary.

STATEMENT OF THE HONORABLE JOHN F. KERRY, SECRETARY OF STATE, U.S. DEPARTMENT OF STATE

Secretary KERRY. Well thank you very much, Chairman Royce, Ranking Member Engel, all the members of the committee. It is my privilege to be here today. I am glad to have this opportunity.

Let me begin by both congratulating you and thanking you for the vote that took place yesterday. We are enormously appreciative, because stepping up the efforts with respect to the moderate opposition is an essential piece of any strategy against ISIL. And I will go into that a little bit in a moment.

I know the chairman knows I have a hard stop on this because I have to be at the White House for a meeting with President Poroshenko. So I will try to really abbreviate, and I will try to keep my answers short. But I also want to make sure I answer your questions sufficiently.

You know, for more than 10 years Iraq has been a source of debate and some disagreement, obviously, up on the Hill, and in the country. I think we waste time today if we focus on rehashing past debates when the issue that confronts us is really straightforward and one on which we ought to all agree. ISIL has to be defeated, plain and simple, end of story. Has to be. And collectively, I think every single one of us is going to be measured by what we do in order to guarantee that that happens.

And the same is true on the international level. Even in a region that has been virtually defined by division over these past years, leaders who couldn't find any agreement for 11 years, and who agree on very little in general, are all in agreement that ISIL has to be defeated.

We have been focused on ISIL, I will tell you, since it morphed into al-Qaeda in Iraq in 2013 and picked up AQI's mission under a different banner. And obviously, prior to that we were focused on it in the full context of what we were doing with respect to al-Qaeda.

In January, we ramped up our assistance to the Iraqi Security Forces, increasing our intelligence, surveillance, reconnaissance, ISR, and flights, to get a better picture of the battlefield and in order to expedite weapons like the Hellfire missiles for the Iraqis so that they could bring those to bear in the fight. Early this summer the ISIL threat accelerated when it effectively obliterated the Iraq-Syria border and the Mosul dam fell.

And there are complicated reasons for why that happened. It is not just a straightforward, you know, they ran over them deal. It has to do with the kind of army that Prime Minister Maliki began to create. It has to do with Shia and Sunni. It has to do with a lot of other ingredients.

But as a result of that, we further surged our ISR missions immediately over Iraq. We immediately set up joint operation centers in Baghdad and Irbil. And our Special Forces immediately conducted a very detailed assessment of the Iraqi Security Forces, because we needed to know, in order to be able to answer your questions and the questions of the American people, what might we be getting into here? Do we have an Iraqi Army that is capable of fighting? To what degree? What will it take to reconstitute it? So whatever judgments are coming to you now are coming to you as a consequence of that assessment.

And in addition to that, I am proud to say that thanks to American engagement, ISIL's movement, which was rapid at that point in time, and perilous, was stopped. Together with the Peshmerga and the brave, courageous souls, the Kurds who stood up, we were able not only to stop them there, but to liberate Amerli, which had been under siege, to liberate Sinjar Mountain, to begin to bring our efforts to bear on Haditha dam, and to make a difference.

By the time ISIL had launched its offensive in the north, President Obama began air strikes, to begin with on the humanitarian basis to protect American personnel and prevent major catastrophes, such as the fall of Haditha dam or the maintenance of the Mosul dam, and also to bolster the Iraqi Security Forces and the Kurdish forces.

To date, we have launched more than 150 air strikes. I know that sounds like that is very few compared to the 16,000 that was mentioned earlier. But it is a different deal right now, because I believe we rightfully, absolutely needed to get in place a structured, clear, Iraqi-chosen, Iraqi effort that provided a government with which we could work going forward. If you didn't have a government with which you could work going forward, nothing that we tried to do would have had the impact necessary.

So, you know, the platforms we put in place last June have enabled us to be able to do what we have done now and there is absolute clarity to the fact that we have blunted ISIL's momentum, created the time and space to be able to put together a comprehensive strategy, get the inclusive government, and build the broad coalition. And that is the way we ought to go at this.

We have redoubled our efforts to move the Iraqi political process forward. We are clear-eyed about the fact that any strategy against ISIL is only going to succeed if it has this strong and inclusive government in Iraq. I hope you noticed the photograph on the front page of the Wall Street Journal 2 days ago that showed Prince Saud al-Faisal, the foreign minister of Saudi Arabia, arm in arm with the Kurdish President of Iraq and with the Shia foreign minister of Iraq. They all came together in Jeddah.

And that is why I went to Baghdad last week, to meet with this new Iraqi Government and make certain of what they were willing to do and were committing to us, and encourage them to discuss in detail their commitment against ISIL, and especially their commitment to unify the country and do the things that haven't been done for these 8 years or more.

What happened in Jeddah was literally historic in terms of the recent history of Iraq and the conflicts of that region. Iraq is now no longer isolated from its neighbors. Last week, the Iraqis weren't just invited to come to Jeddah, but they were warmly received by the Saudis and by the rest of the countries there and the Saudis announced in that meeting that they will reopen an Embassy in Baghdad. That is a big deal. And it is essential.

President Obama outlined the broader strategy in detail the other day. I am not going to go through it all. But I just quickly highlight it because it is important to continually remember this is not just an American effort, number one. And number two, it is not just military, not just kinetic even within the military. It is critical that, you know, we all understand how complicated it is precisely because we are not just focused on taking out the enemy out on the battlefield, but we have to take out an entire network.

I don't know how many of you saw it, but the Australians today arrested a large group of people that they suspected of being ISIL members, supporters, sympathizers in Australia who were planning some kind of extravaganza of brutality in Australia. So we have to decimate and discredit a militant cult masquerading as a religious movement and claiming, with no legitimacy whatsoever, to be a state.

And there are similarities to what we have been doing with al-Qaeda these last years, but frankly it is different for some of the reasons that Chairman Royce pointed out. These folks have now taken over territory in ways that al-Qaeda never did. They have access to money in ways that al-Qaeda never did. They have access to weapons that they captured from Iraqis. And they are holding that territory and beginning to try to build a capacity for sustainability that challenges everybody.

So certainly military support is going to be one component of this. And I sit here today, while I can't go into all of the details at this particular moment for a lot of obvious reasons, I am here to tell you that we have people in Europe committed to being part of kinetic effort, outside of Europe and other parts of the world committed, and in the region, Arab commitments to be part of this effort.

In Syria, the on the ground combat will be done by the moderate opposition, which is Syria's best counterweight to extremists like ISIL. And we can talk more about that moderate opposition, what it looks like, who it is, what they are capable of today, what they could be doing as we go forward.

In addition to the military campaign, we obviously need to dry up the illicit funding sources for al-Qaeda. We have to stop the foreign fighters, people with passports from some of your States, people who could return here with experience in fighting in Syria, or Iraq, and come back and engage in activities here. And the evidence of that is not in my saying it. A fighter who was in Syria traversed back through Turkey and other places, came back to Europe, a French sympathizer, went to Brussels and shot four people outside of a synagogue in Brussels.

So I emphasize that when we say in addition there is another major step, and that will be to continue to deliver humanitarian assistance and to make a difference for the people on the ground so that they don't get sucked in by the money that an ISIL can spend or even pay them. In addition, we have a major effort to undertake to repudiate the insulting distortion of Islam that ISIL is spreading.

I was very encouraged to hear yesterday that Saudi Arabia's top clerical entity, 21 clerics, unanimously came out and declared again that terrorism is a heinous crime under sharia law. More importantly, declared that ISIL has nothing to do with Islam, and that it is in fact the order of Satan. And this is vital, because we know that preventing any individual from joining ISIL, from getting to the battlefield in the first place is actually the most effective measure that we can take.

The top, the grand mufti of Saudi Arabia last week said that ISIL is the number one enemy of Islam. And it might serve us all well to focus on it not in a name that gives it a state, but to focus on it as the enemy of Islam. That is why I spent the last days in Europe and in the Middle East building this coalition, together with other countries.

And that is why I will be in New York tomorrow at the U.N. Security Council at a session that is aimed to build up this coalition even more, and to get even more specific about commitments from each country as to what they are going to do. We have more than 50 countries now contributing in one way or another, with specific understanding of what those countries will do. Some will provide ammunition, some will help with the delegitimizing, some will engage in definancing, some will engage in military assistance, some in training and assistance, some in kinetic activities.

In addition, in New York with me tomorrow will be General John Allen. I think many of you know him. Command in Afghanistan for 2 years, 2011–2013, and deputy commander of Anbar in Iraq and great experience in the region, great respect in the region. Knowledge of the Sunni tribes, of all the folks there that are part of the mix to be able to mobilize action. And he can help us match up each country's capabilities with the needs of the coalition.

And that is another reason why we can't lay it all out to you today because in the Pentagon, as well as in our intel community, as well as the White House, we are marrying all of the needs with the particular coalition contributors.

Ambassador Brett McGurk, as well as Assistant Secretary Anne Patterson, who is so much of a part of the effort against al-Qaeda in Pakistan, are also leading the team. And I commit to you that we will continue to build and enhance the coalition well beyond UNGA.

So with that, I look forward to your questions, and I hope we can get through as much as possible.

Thank you, Mr. Chairman.

[The prepared statement of Secretary Kerry follows:]

Secretary Kerry's Opening Statement
HFAC Hearing on the ISIL Threat

Chairman Royce, Ranking Member Engel, and Members of the Committee, thank
you for holding this hearing on an issue where the stakes are so high and a full
understanding of the ISIL threat and our strategy for defeating it is so important.

And before we begin, I'd like to congratulate you and your colleagues in the House
of Representatives for the strong, bipartisan vote you took last night to authorize
the President's request to train and equip the moderate Syrian opposition. This is
an essential piece of our strategy against ISIL – one I'll get into a bit more in just a
moment – and we are very grateful for your support.

During the years I had the privilege of serving in the U.S. Senate, working with
different Administrations, it always struck me that American foreign policy works
best when there's a genuine discussion, a dialogue, a vetting of ideas back and
forth between Congress and the executive branch. So I want to make sure that by
the time we're done here today, I've heard from you, you've shared your views
and ideas, and that you also have a clear understanding of what we've done so far,
what we're doing now, and where we go next – because your input and your
support are absolutely critical to the success of this effort.

I want to underscore at the start – there are some debates of the past 20 years that
could and probably will fill up books and documentaries for a long time. Iraq is
one.

Iraq has caused some of the most heated debates and deepest divisions of the past
decade – a series of difficult issues about which people can honestly disagree. But
I didn't come here today to rehash those debates. The issue that confronts us today
is one on which we should all agree: ISIL must be defeated. Period. End of story.
And, collectively, we're all going to be measured by how we carry out this
mission.

I'd also underscore – the same is true on an international level. And even in a
region that is virtually defined by division, leaders who have viewed the last 11
years very differently – and who agree on very little in general – are more unified
on this subject than just about any other.

So as President Obama described last week when he spoke directly to the
American people, we have a clear strategy to degrade, defeat and destroy ISIL.

But the United States will not go it alone. That is why we are building a global coalition. And as I traveled around the world this week, the question foreign leaders were asking me was not whether they should join the coalition, but how they can help.

We are also not starting from scratch. This is an effort we have been building over time, both on our own and with the help of our international partners: Even before President Obama delivered his speech last week, nearly 40 countries had joined in contributing to the effort to strengthen the capacity of Iraq including military assistance, training and humanitarian assistance.

We have been focused on ISIL since its inception as the successor to AQI in 2013. Back in January we ramped up our assistance to the Iraqi Security Forces, increasing our intelligence surveillance reconnaissance, or ISR, flights to get a better picture of the battlefield and expediting weapons like Hellfire missiles for the Iraqis to bring to bear in this fight.

Early this summer, the ISIL threat accelerated when it effectively erased the Iraq-Syria border and the Mosul Dam fell. The President acted deliberately and decisively. We further surged our ISR missions over Iraq. We immediately set up joint operation centers in Baghdad and Erbil. And our special forces conducted a very detailed field assessment of Iraqi Security Forces and Kurdish forces.

By the time ISIL launched the offensive in the north, President Obama authorized limited air strikes against ISIL and humanitarian missions to protect American personnel, prevent major catastrophes and support Iraqi Security Forces and Kurdish forces that were fighting bravely to do the same. To date, we've launched more than 150 airstrikes. And it is because of the platforms we put in place back in June that those strikes have been highly precise and incredibly effective, including in the operations to break the siege of Sinjar Mountain, retake Mosul Dam, and resupply the town of Amerli.

These actions blunted ISIL's momentum and created time and space for us to put in place the two pillars of a comprehensive strategy against ISIL: an inclusive Iraq government, and a broad international coalition.

We redoubled our efforts to help move the Iraqi political process forward. We were clear-eyed about the fact that any strategy against ISIL would only succeed with a strong, inclusive government in Iraq, with an ambitious national agenda, prepared to unite the country against ISIL.

With our support, after several weeks of complex negotiations, President Masum nominated Haider al-Abadi to serve as Prime Minister. Shortly thereafter, Prime Minister al-Abadi – again with our support – was able to form his cabinet and present it to the parliament, and, last week, that government was approved.

This was a long and difficult process, led by the Iraqis, with our help as needed. The result was something Iraq had never before seen in its history: an election deemed credible by the United Nations, followed by peaceful transition of power, without any US troops on the ground.

I traveled to Baghdad last week, immediately after the new government was approved, to meet with Prime Minister al-Abadi and other leaders throughout the Iraqi government. And I was very encouraged to hear them discuss in detail the government's National Plan to unite the country against ISIL, and empower local communities – particularly in Sunni areas – to mobilize, defeat ISIL, and maintain security control in their area.

Throughout the entire process, we were in touch with regional leaders to ensure that a new and inclusive government would receive support from the region. Today, after years, even decades, of relative isolation from their neighbors, the Iraqis have begun to reintegrate with the broader Arab community. For example, last week, they were not just invited but warmly welcomed in Saudi Arabia, and the Saudis have now said they'll reopen an embassy in Baghdad.

With this new, inclusive Iraqi government in place, it's time for the defensive strategy we and our international partners have pursued thus far to transition to an offensive strategy – one that harnesses the capabilities of the entire world to eliminate the ISIL threat, once and for all.

President Obama outlined this strategy in detail, so – while I am happy to answer any questions you may have – I will be brief in walking through it again now.

At its core, our strategy is centered on a global coalition that will collaborate closely across a number of specific areas – including, certainly, on direct and indirect military support.

To be clear, military assistance comes in a range of forms, from training and equipping, to logistics and airlift. And countries from inside and outside of the region are already providing support in these veins. So I have no doubt whatsoever we will have the capabilities and the resources we need to succeed militarily. And President Obama made clear we will be expanding the military campaign to take on ISIL in Iraq, in Syria – wherever it is found.

But this is not the Gulf War in 1991, and it is not the Iraq War in 2003 – for a couple of reasons. Number one, U.S. ground troops will not be sent into combat in this conflict. From the last decade we know that a sustainable strategy is not U.S. ground forces – it is enabling local forces to do what they must for themselves and their country. I want to be clear: the U.S. troops that have been deployed to Iraq do not and will not have a combat mission. Instead, they will support Iraqi forces on the ground as they fight for their own country against these terrorists.

And in Syria, the on-the-ground combat will be done by the moderate opposition – which serves as the best counter-weight in Syria to extremists like ISIL. We know that as ISIL gets weaker, this moderate opposition will get stronger, which will be critical in our efforts to bring about the political solution necessary to address the crisis in Syria once and for all. That's one of the reasons why we're so grateful that the House of Representatives yesterday authorized the opposition train-and-equip mission, and why it's so critical that the Senate do the same. But it's also critical that the opposition makes the most of this additional support – the kind of support they've been requesting for years – and take this opportunity to prove to the world that they can be a viable alternative to Assad.

Number two, this is more than just a military coalition because the objective requires more than a military victory. This mission isn't just about taking out an enemy on the battlefield. It's about taking out an entire network – decimating and discrediting a militant cult masquerading as a religious movement.

It's similar to what we have been doing to Al Qaeda these last years.

The bottom line is we will not be successful with a military campaign alone. Nor are we asking every country to play a military role – we don't need every country to play a military role and we don't want every country to play a military role.

Only a holistic campaign can accomplish our objectives. That is why we are focused on multiple lines of effort.

In addition to the military campaign, it will be equally important for the global coalition to dry up ISIL's illicit funding, to stop the foreign fighters who carry passports from countries around the world including the United States, to continue to deliver urgently needed humanitarian assistance, and finally, to repudiate the gross distortion of Islam that ISIL is spreading, and put an end to the sermons by extremists that brainwash young men to join these movements and commit mass atrocities in the name of God. I was very encouraged to hear that Saudi Arabia's top clerics came out and declared terrorism a "heinous crime" under Sharia law – and that perpetrators should be made an example of. Preventing an individual from joining ISIL for example, or from getting to the battle field in the first place, is the most effective measure we can take.

I want to emphasize – when we say "global coalition," we mean it. This is not a threat that a single country or region can take on alone. And there is a critical role for nearly every country to play.

So we are committed to working with countries in every corner of the globe to match the campaign's requirements with the capabilities they are willing to bring to bear. I spent the past week in the Middle East and in Europe, meeting with dozens of leaders whose partnership will be essential to our success.

And I can tell you today: every single person I spoke to over the course of my trip expressed strong support for our mission and a willingness to help in some way. We had excellent meetings, beginning at the NATO Summit in Wales, and then in Jeddah. The Jeddah Communique represents a strong, comprehensive and unified statement of all the ways in which the region is committed to supporting this fight. Our meetings in Baghdad, in Cairo, and in Ankara also advanced the process. And at the conference earlier this week in Paris, we took another step along the road to the UNGA and the UNSC sessions next week.

We have a plan and we know the players. Our focus now is determining what role each country will play.

Later this week we will have more to say about our partners and contributions, and we fully expect the coalition to grow, evolve and coalesce well beyond UNGA. That's why we've asked one of our most respected and experienced military leaders – General John Allen – to come to the State Department and oversee this effort. And he's already hitting the ground running – he was at work last Friday at 7:00 am, less than 24 hours after we sealed the deal for him to do this job, and he and I had a long meeting yesterday, just a few hours after I landed in DC. General Allen will be working with one of our foremost Iraq experts, Ambassador Brett McGurk, as well as Assistant Secretary Anne Patterson, who was so much a part of the effort against Al Qaeda when she was our Ambassador in Pakistan.

The fact is that, if we do this right, then this effort could become a global model for isolating and undermining other extremist threats around the world. But now we must be laser focused on ISIL. And I'm confident that, with our strategy in place and our international partners by our side, we will have all that we need to succeed in degrading and ultimately destroying this monstrous organization – wherever it exists.

###

Chairman ROYCE. And I think that does bring up a good question, Mr. Secretary, which is how we move forward to get a large portion of this paid for by Saudi Arabia, by Kuwait.

I remember in 1990, when the invasion of Kuwait occurred, in order to push that army, which at the time was the fifth largest army in the world, the Iraqi Army, in order to push it out of Kuwait there was a coalition and there were 116,000 air strikes that decimated 42 divisions. Frankly, the tanks, 3,700 were destroyed, the armored vehicles were destroyed. We saw the value of air power in pushing back a force. And to date I think we have less than 200 air strikes. So that is one point I would bring up with you.

Another point I would bring up just goes to the question of what we can do with respect to those passports you spoke of, French, Belgian, British, Australian. These are individuals who would be able to travel to the United States without a visa. I know that we have the authority here in the United States, State Department can revoke a passport if someone is likely to cause serious damage to the national security of the United States. But we frankly need some kind of interagency process I think to identify westerners that travel to fight alongside ISIL. And I wanted to speak to you about that issue as well. I have been working on legislation to address this.

We should have a carve out, of course, for Doctors Without Borders, and the doctors group SAMS, and other groups that are going to try to help with respect to setting up hospitals in refugee camps. But in terms of those going to fight, I think we need a way to approach this to make certain that their ability to come back into the United States is made a hell of a lot more difficult than it is right now.

And I want to ask you, Mr. Secretary, about that.

Secretary KERRY. Yes, sir. Chairman Royce, let me just say very quickly it is just not the time to begin comparing the number of air strikes, because the number of air strikes that took place, obviously then, was related to an invasion, a full-scale invasion. This is not an invasion. This is a counterterrorism operation. And it is going to be different, number one.

Number two, if we had engaged in just jumping in and leaping in and doing air strikes one place or another without the structure, without the forethought or the proper targeting and so forth and something went awry, we would be up here, and every single one of you would be looking at us and asking us why we shot before we aimed and did our homework.

Chairman ROYCE. But Mr. Secretary, with all due respect on that point, our ability now with armed drones and with F–16s to be able to see a target from the air——

Secretary KERRY. I agree.

Chairman ROYCE [continuing]. We could actually see from the planes the fact that they were flying this black flag, they were in long columns. We didn't know what was happening here. They took Fallujah, you know, they took Tikrit, they eventually took Mosul, and in every one of these situations we had an opportunity to hit those columns from the air.

Secretary KERRY. Mr. Chairman, you are absolutely correct. And I will tell you I was chomping at the bit and agonizing over that watching these convoys. And you would see them on CNN and say why aren't we doing this?

But in point of fact, when we stopped and thought through the strategy, if we had begun to do that and did it in full swing, we might have actually interrupted, if not prevented, the capacity of the Iraqi Government to have a new government and new formation. And there were serious considerations there about the timing and——

Chairman ROYCE. And I acknowledge that point, but at the same time, by the time this got to Mosul, and we are talking now about the central bank in Mosul, we had reached a point where the ability to take that city and take the cash out of the central bank would arm this terrorist organization to an extent that no terrorist organization previously had their hands on that much cash.

Secretary KERRY. That is why we are building the coalition, Chairman, because they have to buy those weapons from somewhere. That cash has got to go out to another country, it has to go out through a system. Somehow those weapons have got to get in there. And if we do this effectively enough, and that is where all countries can play a role, shutting their borders, enforcing the law, engaging in intel cooperation, and preventing that money from being effective if you can't spend it effectively out of the country. Now, that is one.

Two, with respect to passports, you are absolutely correct, I have the authority to revoke passports. And we are currently examining all of the people, the individuals. We are trying to learn as well as we can who is there and what those possibilities are. We also need to do that with sensitivity to certain investigations that may be going on because you don't want to flag something.

Chairman ROYCE. I understand.

Secretary KERRY. But we are well aware. That is part of the strategy and part of the process. And what I want to make certain is that anybody who has a passport who returns, returns in handcuffs, not through Customs with their passport. And that is our goal. Finally——

Chairman ROYCE. My time has expired. Finally, you can finish, Mr. Secretary.

Secretary KERRY. No, no, that is fine.

Chairman ROYCE. My only point here was we have to step it up from the air.

Let's go to Mr. Elliott Engel from New York.

Mr. ENGEL. Thank you, Mr. Chairman.

Mr. Secretary, there have been several falsehoods and misrepresentations of the moderate opposition, and particularly the Free Syria Army.

I would like to clarify one point. The Free Syria Army is committed to fighting ISIL. I would like to request unanimous consent to place in the record a statement by General Bashir, the chief of staff of the supreme military command of the Free Syrian Army, in which he states that the Free Syrian Army is committed to fighting ISIL.

I want to just quickly read part of his statement:

''As chief of staff of the supreme military command, I hereby reaffirm the Free Syria Army's continued commitment to removing the twin terrorists Bashar al-Assad and Abu Bakr Al-Baghdadi from Syrian soil. The heroes of the Free Syrian Army have sacrificed thousands of brave souls in the fight against the imposter Islamic State over the past year. We fully plan to continue this fight until Baghdadi's complete and utter defeat. The Assad regime collaborates with Islamic State and other terrorist groups like Hezbollah that seek our extermination. We will be unable to finish off Islamic State without also acting to stop Assad's barbaric assaults.

''We call upon the world community, and the U.S. Congress in particular, to fulfill the humanitarian security responsibilities by providing the Free Syrian Army with robust support to bring a Syria free from terrorism in all its forms.''

So I would like to put that into the record, Mr. Chairman.

As the FSA fights ISIL, we must remember that Assad remains a magnet for terrorists and foreign fighters. So there will be no stabilization of this conflict unless Assad is forced to stop his barbaric slaughter of his own people.

So I would like to ask you, Mr. Secretary, for comments on what I just said, and to clarify what you meant by the United States deconflicting with the Assad regime. What do you expect our policy toward the Assad regime to be?

And additionally, it appears that Assad's forces have encircled Aleppo, and that the moderate opposition is losing its ability to hold territory there. And knowing that Assad has employed a kneel or starve campaign, compelling his opposition to either surrender or die, and that Aleppo has symbolic importance as a rebel stronghold, what can the U.S. do to help prevent the starvation of the moderate opposition inside Aleppo and help them hold Aleppo?

Secretary KERRY. Well, thank you, Congressman Engel.

First of all, thank you for your leadership, and Chairman Royce, thank you for your leadership. You guys have been pushing on this, and you have been very articulate about the needs with respect to the Syrian opposition. And we appreciate that. And I appreciate the comments you just made.

Indeed, the Syrian opposition is in the tens of thousands. I can't tell you precisely exactly how many. But sufficient that they are a legitimate force. And the principal political arm of the opposition is the Syrian Opposition Coalition, the political arm, which is a group of people who represent the various parts of it. The SOC includes representatives of the Free Syrian Army and when possible, they have been able to provide funding and supplies to the fighting forces.

The fighting forces are a conglomerate of armed groups that were formed to defend local communities from regime attacks and it includes secular as well as some Islamists. But the Islamist elements are opposed to ISIL and al-Nusra.

We have very specific numbers in certain movements, like the Hazzm movement, is about 4,000 fighters divided into certain divisions. There are regimist defectors who have come in who are also part of this effort.

There are other groups, at least seven groups with somewhere between a couple of thousand and 4,000 fighters each. But that is not all of the moderate forces by any means. And what is important is all of these forces have a solid record of fighting ISIL. They have been fighting ISIL. They are fighting ISIL right now up around Aleppo and in other areas.

In fact, they drove out ISIL from Idlib province. In Deir al-Zour, another area in the Damascus suburbs, they have been fighting. And the thinking is that without prompting from outside forces, without America coming in and saying we are helping to fight ISIL, they are fighting ISIL.

So we believe that as this global coalition comes together, determined to take on ISIL, that the organizing principle of the region, which is success breeds success, you are going to begin to see more people say we are on the side of the moderates, we are going to be with the moderates. They will grow in strength. And we can begin, indeed, to isolate ISIL itself.

Aleppo is still under siege, obviously. ISIL is trying to gain control of some border crossings. But helping those units right now around Aleppo actually could help us secure supply routes from Turkey and raise the moderate fighter morale in significant ways. The moderate opposition is also fighting al-Nusra, especially in Idlib Province. And our sense, again, is that on occasion there has been a kind of tactical cooperation purely for sort of immediate purposes. But to our judgment and the judgment of our people, it has had no lasting kind of impact.

So our feeling is, Congressman, that we have something to work with here. I am not telling you it is easy. I am not going to tell you that it will happen all overnight. But there is indeed the Syrian opposition, which you have been arguing for a number of years, which notwithstanding the absence of a full throated support structure has survived and continues to fight. And our judgment is they will now even moreso.

Chairman ROYCE. Ileana Ros-Lehtinen is chair of the Subcommittee on the Middle East and North Africa.

Ms. ROS-LEHTINEN. Thank you so much, Mr. Chairman and ranking member.

Welcome, Mr. Secretary.

I have reservations about the President's plan to train and equip the so-called moderate Syrian rebels. The President doesn't have the will to do all that is necessary in Iraq and Syria. And the result is the half measure that we passed yesterday, which tells our enemies what we won't do. Does the President have this comprehensive plan to not only defeat ISIL but also other terrorist groups—you just referred to al-Nusra—and remove Assad from power? Or do we no longer view Assad staying in power as an impediment?

Ambassador Power said recently that there were discrepancies and omissions in Assad's declaration regarding the removal and destruction of his chemical weapons stockpile. Assad did not live up to his obligations, and ISIL may use these, if it gets access to these weapons. Does Assad still have hidden, undeclared poison gases and chemical weapons? We have already seen that ISIL seized a former chemical weapons depot in Iraq and it would be a nightmare scenario if it were to also get Assad's undeclared chemical weapons.

Also, Mr. Secretary, reports suggest that ISIL fighters number in the 30,000 to 40,000 range, different reports. Given its sophistication and its force strength, how can we expect a few thousand Syrian rebels to fight against ISIL and Assad at the same time?

We know that some of our top and former military leaders have said that a time may come when we may have to put boots on the ground to supplement the Kurds, the Iraqi forces, the so-called moderate Syrian rebels. But this has been repeatedly rebuffed by the President. Our allies in the gulf need to make substantive investments for the coalition. Has any country pledged or indicated that should the need arise it will be willing to send its own troops on the ground in Syria?

And lastly, a point on the misguided Iran nuclear deal, why the double standard with Syria and Iran? We have rightfully demanded that Syria dismantle, destroy, and remove its chemical weapons program, however imperfectly. But we are allowing Iran to keep its nuclear program infrastructure intact with enrichment capabilities and thousands of centrifuges spinning.

Thank you, sir.

Secretary KERRY. There is a lot of meat there, and I obviously can't get through all of it now, but I am happy to answer what we can in writing.

Assad's legitimacy? No. There is no legitimacy. We still believe that there is no way that we would imagine the support for those who have been taking on Assad is simply not going to stop. And so there is only a political solution here. And we don't see how that has Assad with some long term future in Syria. Besides, even as they are willing to fight ISIL, the Syrian opposition is not going to stop continuing to fight Assad. So we recognize that reality.

Secondly, with respect to poison gas, we actually accomplished something historic to many people's skepticism about its possibilities. And that is that all of the declared prohibited chemicals under the Convention have been removed and destroyed. All of them. That has never happened, particularly in a time of conflict, in any country in the world. And I am very proud of the effort made by the folks who are arriving today in Virginia on the Cape Ray Merchant Marine, and the Navy and the other folks who were all involved in helping to achieve that goal.

Ms. ROS-LEHTINEN. If I may, Mr. Secretary, so when Samantha Power says there are discrepancies and omissions——

Secretary KERRY. I was just going to come to that. She is right. Those are declared materials. Chlorine is not a required declared material. And we also have some questions about a couple of other items. Those are being prosecuted or, you know, being pursued within the process.

And indeed, we believe there is evidence of Assad's use of chlorine, which when you use it, despite it not being on the list, is prohibited under the Chemical Weapons Convention. So he is in violation of that agreement. And we believe, and we are proceeding to do things to——

Ms. ROS-LEHTINEN. Thank you, sir. And I have some written questions regarding Venezuela sanctions and security for Camp Liberty at another time.

Secretary KERRY. Delighted. Thank you.

Chairman ROYCE. Without objection.

Mr. Faleomavaega of American Samoa, ranking member of the Asia Subcommittee.

Mr. FALEOMAVAEGA. Thank you, Mr. Chairman.

Mr. Secretary, the ISIS organization has caught the international community off guard. What began as a movement in tribal lands and minor outlying provinces is now a worldwide threat. Only after two beheadings did President Obama announce his strategy to, and I quote, ''degrade and ultimately destroy the Islamic State organization.'' While I appreciate your presence here today, Mr. Secretary, I cannot underscore the importance of Congress's role in determining how the United States responds to this crisis.

What we do and how we do it now is the main issue. We must act responsibly and swiftly. And we must have true and accurate facts and information so that we can assure the American people that our actions in the region are not only warranted, but just. We must act and get this thing correctly.

You mentioned in your statement, Mr. Secretary, that ISIS has to be defeated. And you have also outlined some aspects of the administration's efforts to fulfill this problem. As veterans ourselves in the Vietnam war, are we looking at another Vietnam, Mr. Secretary, if we don't get this right?

Secretary KERRY. No. Because we are not invading the country. We are not going to be getting in the middle of a civil war. We are going to be part of a coalition that is engaged in counterterrorism. This is a counterterrorist operation, not counterinsurgency, and certainly not engagement in a civil war.

Mr. FALEOMAVAEGA. Is there a concern among the neighboring countries in the region about what is happening as far as the operations and what the crisis organization has done? My point is that are the Arab countries supportive of us and our efforts to address this serious issue?

Secretary KERRY. Hugely. Hugely supportive. That is what the Jeddah conference is about. We had all of the members of the Gulf Cooperation Council there, together with Lebanon, and Jordan, Iraq, and Turkey.

And they all joined in a major condemnation, unified, about ISIL and what it is doing. And look, without seeking it, we obviously all know that on the surface, though he doesn't have the ability or the will to do anything about it, Assad doesn't like them. And Iran doesn't like them. Russia doesn't like them. Russia, which is supporting Assad. So you have a confluence of obviously strange bed fellows, which doesn't promise cooperation, because we are not engaging in that, but all of them are opposed and I think people are clearly distinguishing between ISIL and other political issues of the region.

Mr. FALEOMAVAEGA. You and I both know that rhetoric is very easy to come up with. Are they also committing resources to address this issue?

Secretary KERRY. Yes. I am not going to run through them all now. But there are a lot of countries—40 countries have already sent in ammunition, provided money, engaged in humanitarian assistance. They are already engaged. We have a couple of nations that are already flying with us, though we haven't, obviously, you know, made major pronouncements about where the whole coalition is because we are still in the process, as I said earlier, of delineating who will do what, when, where, and how.

Mr. FALEOMAVAEGA. As a wounded combat veteran, Mr. Secretary yourself, in the Vietnam war, I cannot think of a better person that really appreciates and understands the importance that when we send our men, soldiers and sailors, at the expense of their lives, that we need to make this thing right. And we don't need another Vietnam, in my opinion.

Thank you, Mr. Chairman.

Chairman ROYCE. Thank you.

We go now to Mr. Chris Smith of New Jersey.

Mr. SMITH. Thank you very much, Mr. Chairman.

Mr. Secretary, welcome.

Secretary KERRY. Thank you.

Mr. SMITH. First of all, I want to thank you for your strong August 28 statement calling on Iran to release Saeed Abedini, Amir Hekmati, and to locate Robert Levinson. Perhaps you might want to tell us if there has been any response. But I do, and I know other members, are very grateful for that strong statement.

Secondly, do the Leahy amendments, will they be vigorously applied to the vetting process?

Secretary KERRY. Yes.

Mr. SMITH. Okay.

And third, over a year ago I wrote an op-ed published in the Washington Post calling for the creation of a war crimes tribunal for Syria, the idea being that there needs to be accountability for all sides, regardless of whoever commits the atrocities, and it needs to be done and set up and established immediately.

A resolution calling for the immediate establishment of the tribunal was passed by this committee and awaits floor action. I argued then, and I would argue now, that the ICC, which has already had a thumbs down by the Russians, is not up to the task.

David Crane, who as you know was the chief prosecutor of the Sierra Leone War Crimes Tribunal, testified here and said that the ICC is not up to the task. It has had only one conviction in about a dozen years. And that was of a person committing atrocities in the Democratic Republic of Congo. But the idea behind a hybrid, or a, you know, tribunal like Yugoslavia and Sierra Leone and Rwanda, would be that all sides would be held to account.

Milosevic, as we all know, died while his trial was going on. Mladic and Karadzic are currently under—you know, their trials are continuing. Nobody thought at the time that Charles Taylor would get 50 years, the former President of Liberia. And I will never forget that picture of him after the verdict was read, looking down. Here is the man who, as you know and I know and others, and we fought against him for so long, the atrocities that he committed in Liberia and Sierra Leone. He is in jail now for 50 years.

This would be an accountability initiative. It needs to be stood up immediately. And I respectfully hope that the administration will do just that.

I yield.

Secretary KERRY. Well, let me begin, Congressman, first of all, you are tireless and persistent in your advocacy for these things. And we all respect that enormously, number one.

Number two, every occasion that we get, even most recently in Geneva at the meeting in the context of the P5+1, we raise the issue of our folks who are being held. And I can't go into all of it here now except to tell you that we are actively pursuing some way of trying to see whether or not both countries' needs can't be met. As you can imagine, they have counter demands. And we are engaged in looking at that. But we are very much engaged. We have had various efforts for proof of life, we have had various discussions with other countries in the region. And this is very much on our minds. And the President will not rest when any American citizen is held like that and it remains unresolved.

With respect to the tribunal, I personally, when I was in the Senate, I helped to work on the special U.N. tribunal that held the Khmer Rouge responsible for their atrocities. There is no question in my mind that what has happened in Syria, on a number of occasions the government has engaged in war crimes. And I think they need to be held accountable. And I very much support it.

The President supports finding a mechanism that will do that. I don't know if we have made the same judgment that some have with respect to the inability of the current structure to do it. But we ought to try to resolve this one way or the other. It shouldn't be sitting in limbo. People need to know there is accountability. And one of the problems historically, as you know better than anybody, is the impunity that exists. If there is impunity in one country, in one area, one region, continent, or another, people tend to try to get away with things. It is the prosecution that acts as a deterrent, it is the accountability that stops it. And we will work with you to try to provide that.

Chairman ROYCE. We go now to Mr. Sherman of California, ranking member of the Subcommittee on Terrorism, Nonproliferation, and Trade.

Mr. SHERMAN. Mr. Secretary, I have got so much to cover, some of the questions you may want to respond to for the record.

First, I want to commend the administration for its success in dealing with Assad's chemical weapons. As you have pointed out, you may be 90 percent successful, you may be 99 percent successful, but there was no other plan presented that would have freed the world from the risk posed by the vast majority of Assad's chemical weapons.

I want to commend the chair and the ranking member for their opening statements, particularly the ranking member when he mentioned the Free Syria Act. I was happy to be an original co-sponsor of that 1½ years ago. And the ranking member is correct, we need to write a new authorization to use military force and replace the ones we have now.

Whether or not your air campaign, Mr. Secretary, is legally authorized, depends upon whether ISIS is part of al-Qaeda. That is a metaphysical question. They weren't in existence on September 11, 2001. Then they were formed. Then they joined al-Qaeda. And then they left al-Qaeda. And now they are fighting al-Qaeda. I don't know if they are part of al-Qaeda or not. It is a metaphysical question. The solution is for Congress to write a statute that fits 2015 rather than see whether you can stretch a 2001 statute to fit a circumstance that was never anticipated.

Mr. Secretary, the American people want a great plan. We want a guarantee of the immediate, total destruction of ISIS, without U.S. casualties. And the administration will be pilloried for not developing such a plan. I want to commend you for not giving in to the political pressure to promise what cannot be delivered.

In your statement you said we would defeat ISIS. I know the President's words are eventually defeat ISIS. To listen to some pundits, you would think that not only do we have to totally and immediately destroy ISIS, but we have to do so without discussions with questionable allies. And the Middle East has almost no allies except questionable allies. The fact is that can be done if we are willing to put ½ million troops on the ground the way—or at least several hundred thousand troops on the ground and incur the casualties that none of the pundits is willing to discuss.

But it also ignores another situation. It is not just who you destroy, it is who you empower. And ISIS's most powerful opponents, at least most powerful today, are nearly as evil as ISIS, and perhaps more dangerous. Hezbollah, Iran, the extremist Shiite militias that Iran controls, Assad, al-Nusra, a division of al-Qaeda. These are the other powerful forces on the battlefield. And there is a lot of discussion about how ISIS members have passports that might allow them to conduct terrorist operations outside the Middle East.

Hezbollah has killed hundreds of Americans in Lebanon. Iran and Hezbollah have killed hundreds of Americans in Iraq. And both have conducted terrorist activities on a variety of different continents. Mr. Secretary, the Middle East is a region of incredibly complex evil. Caution is not a vice and bravado is not a virtue.

Maliki ignored us, didn't need us. Abadi needs us. I hope that one of the things you bring up with him is his international obligations to protect those who are living at Camp Liberty. Turkey is not fulfilling its responsibilities. And here I do have a question, believe it or not.

One of the problems with Turkey is they are allowing this oil to be smuggled. The question is, and I don't want you to give away any secrets here but is there some reason why we haven't bombed those oil fields and refineries under ISIS control? This would deprive them of money from smuggling. It would deprive them of fuel for their own operations. It would also, unfortunately, deprive civilians under their control of fuel as well.

During World War II we bombed oil fields and refineries even if that meant that enemy civilians couldn't get fuel. Do we have an objection to bombing these oil fields and refineries now?

Secretary KERRY. I haven't heard any objection.

Chairman ROYCE. Why don't we do this, Mr. Secretary.

Why don't I suggest we respond in writing, because the gentleman used all of his time.

Given that circumstance, we will go to Mr. Rohrabacher of California, chair of the Subcommittee on Europe, Eurasia, and Emerging Threats.

Mr. ROHRABACHER. Thank you.

And first of all, let me express my appreciation to you personally, Mr. Secretary. You are working hard, you are doing your best for us. We may have some disagreements, but all of us should appreciate the hard work that you are putting out. And also the respect that you are showing the American people and Congress today by being here and opening yourself up to this type of very energetic questioning.

So I will get to my energetic questioning. Let me understand. The proposal that I seem to be seeing here is that we support the Free Syrian Army, and we build them up, and although it does have some good elements, there is every indication that it is riddled with radical Islamic elements, terrorists, many of whom are more committed to fighting the regime, Assad's regime, than fighting ISIL. And Assad's regime, which of course means us no harm, but they themselves are engaged with fighting ISIL.

In the end, it seems to me we are going to be basically providing weapons in order to undercut an enemy of ISIL, who is engaged deeply in fighting that radical Islamic terrorist element. Am I wrong in that? Am I missing something there?

The dynamic that is created in the end, a big army that—Assad's regime's armed forces that are a major part in the fight against ISIL are going to be undercut by what we are doing?

Secretary KERRY. Regrettably, Congressman, no, we are not going to be undercut. Because if Assad's forces indeed do decide to focus on ISIL significantly, which they haven't been doing throughout this period—I mean there is evidence that Assad has played footsie with them. And he has used them as a tool of weakening the opposition. And therefore, never took on their headquarters, which were there and obvious, and other assets that they had. So we have no confidence that Assad is either capable of or willing to take on ISIL, number one.

So we don't see a conflict in that process. Now, that may develop somewhat depending on how far they get. I think, with respect to the weapons and what is going to them, I am not going to sit here and tell you that the vetting process is a perfect process. But we have gained enormous expertise in the vetting over 20 years.

Mr. ROHRABACHER. Okay.

Secretary KERRY. General Nagata——

Mr. ROHRABACHER. Mr. Secretary——

Secretary KERRY. Let me just say perhaps you guys might invite him up here. I think it would be worth your hearing from him as to exactly how they vet, what they do. We have a lot of relationships with vetted moderate members.

Mr. ROHRABACHER. I think we have a poor track record in determining who our friends are in the past. And vetting, I will have to tell you, Mr. Secretary, the people we rely on for that vetting I don't have any confidence in whatsoever.

Mr. Secretary, the administration inherited a big challenge in the Middle East. The Republican administration left this administration with big problems. And I think that this administration has turned a big challenge into a major crisis and one of the most significant factors in turning this into a crisis is this administration seems unable to go directly to America's best allies and support them, but instead find fault with them, and have basically overseen replacing good allies who were flawed with people who hate us, an expansion of the radical Islamic terrorist movement in that area. The people I know in that region who are the most loyal to us are the Kurds. And yet this administration insists on all of the supplies that were going to were a bulwark against these radicals. All the supplies have to go through Baghdad.

Now, why are we marginalizing our best friends the Kurds and denying them the weapons they need—and they are really on the front line—in order to help the government in Baghdad, who by the way, I think still is allied with the mullah regime in Iran. And in fact here we are contacting the mullah regime to associate with us, but here Assad is a horrible alternative to deal with, but we can deal with the Iranian mullahs. I mean this is contradictory. It seems again our friends are getting short-changed because they are imperfect, and we end up helping our enemies.

Secretary KERRY. Well, Congressman, there are two big points you raise there; and I want to take them both on.

We could not be more engaged with our long-time, good friends throughout the region. I have probably made more trips as Secretary of State to the region and had more conversations in 1½ years than any former Secretary of State.

We just came back from a meeting hosted by one of our foremost, most important, longest allies in the region, Saudi Arabia. There was unanimity at that meeting from all of the folks present, including some you might be referring to who don't have a record of being fully supportive of every effort all the time in that region. But that is not us. That is them.

We have made it clear what our expectations are. And our expectations are that people stop funding Islamic radical groups—Islamic is the wrong word—radical religious extremists.

Mr. ROHRABACHER. Right. Okay.

Secretary KERRY. We need to stop seeing them funded, and we need to start making sure there is a solid support stream and only that stream to the moderate opposition. So we are on the same page.

Chairman ROYCE. We are going to go——

Secretary KERRY. Now, you asked for this—this is important, Mr. Chairman, because maybe you can rectify it. You complain about— you say the administration is responsible for sending all these weapons through Baghdad. No, we are not. You are. We are adhering to U.S. law, passed by Congress with respect to export-import and exports and what we are allowed to do. We have to send it to the Government, because that is U.S. law. If you want to change it to fix it——

Mr. ROHRABACHER. That is why we should recognize the Kurdish Government, well, the sovereign power.

Chairman ROYCE. The time has expired. But that particular point you raise about changing law is one that we could undertake and, given the frustrations of the Kurdish foreign minister, I think it is one we will undertake.

We go now to Mr. Gregory Meeks of New York.

Mr. MEEKS. Thank you, Mr. Chairman.

And thank you, Mr. Secretary, for all the work that you have been doing.

Yesterday I voted in support of the amendment that would authorize the training and equipping of appropriate vetted elements of the Syrian opposition. And I did so because I believe that we can't ignore the threat from ISIL and because, I believe, that the strategy that the President has proposed is probably the best option that is available to us at this time.

But it wasn't an easy vote. It is a very—it was a very difficult vote. And I had to talk to a number of different individuals that reached out to Ambassadors and, of course, attended all of the classified meetings, et cetera, come away with what you said is absolutely key and essential that we have to have—this cannot be seen as the United States against Sunni Muslims.

And so everybody being engaged in more than just words, but actually engaged in this fight, I think, is absolutely important.

But one of the things that I came away with after the vote in talking to members on the floor and in talking all today, there were certain questions that came up. In fact, certain questions were asked here today; and you didn't have a chance to answer. So I thought that I would ask a couple of them, and then be quiet so you could have a chance to answer.

One that continues to happen is the question of a slippery slope. And given that, I know that you understand this because of your service in Vietnam and your talk.

So the question was: How will you assess if this war has gone wrong, if it is going wrong, and why we are not on a slippery slope and what is different this time? So I would like to know that.

Then I think Mr. Engel and Mr. Sherman talked about the AUMF, and so I was wondering if—and I believe that you already have authority that you need, but many want to renew it. So could you or would you be helpful in language on a new AUMF, and are you willing to work with Congress on this matter?

Secretary KERRY. Well, absolutely, Congressman. Thank you very much for both questions. They are very relevant. Very appropriate.

On the slippery slope issue, I think it is ingrained in a lot of us through the past experience of the last 45, 50 years, in some cases, very personally, in other cases, through the experience here in the Congress and through our experience in the Middle East in the last few years.

So we are all fairly warned. We understand the dangers. That is why the President is being so clear. And that is why the President is adamant about building this coalition with the real assumption of responsibility within the coalition, not a hold your coat, we will watch you while you do it, not a fig leaf kind of, you know, we will do a little bit, but a genuine coalition to tackle what is a genuine threat to every one of those countries more immediately in some ways than to us.

Now, that has to happen. And we are going to be very disciplined and very tough about making that kind of assessment; and you are, too—and we know that—in conjunction with each other. So I think we will know fairly rapidly how things are coming together, how effective, what is effective. And we have got a really tough individual seasoned in leadership in these things in John Allen, who will help us make those judgments as we go along.

On the AUMF, we welcome updating the AUMF. We are not trying to avoid that. It would be very good for everybody, I think. And so we welcome it. And, of course, we will work with you, very, very closely in an effort to do that. Chairman Menendez said yesterday that he is, in fact, already proceeding down that road; and we intend to work with him and with all of you in order to be effective. But we are convinced beyond any doubt that we do have the legal authority to proceed now.

Would it be better to have something in 2014 that speaks to this particular situation rather than a 2001 AMF? Sure. But that is not where we are starting. And we need to get moving, and we have been very careful to make the judgments about authority here.

One of the reasons, you know, that we couldn't move without coming to you before was because we didn't have authority, in our judgment, with respect to Syria and chemical weapons because that didn't fall under the 2001 AUMF. So we have clearly drawn that distinction and there is effort to stretch here.

But we will be better, all of us, with Congress, the American people clear about where we are heading.

Chairman ROYCE. We go to Mr. Chabot of Ohio, chairman of the Subcommittee on Asia.

Mr. CHABOT. Thank you, Mr. Chairman.

And thank you for appearing this morning—this afternoon, Mr. Secretary.

Like everybody in this room, I am sure I watched and, I think, a lot of people watched the President. Many, I think, were shocked when he emphasized that the Islamic State of Iraq and the Levant was, in fact, not Islamic. They now simply refer to themselves as the Islamic State. You know, they don't call themselves the Methodist state or Episcopalian state, or the Baptist state. They are the Islamic State and, I think, for good reasons.

You know, when Christians, for example, are told to convert to Islam or die, that would seem to fly in the face of the President's insistence that the Islamic State is not the Islamic State, and an indication that he may not fully accept that radical Islam is, indeed, something that does exist and, in fact, is growing.

Now, let me get to my question. The President has emphasized over and over again that there will be no American boots on the ground. Isn't that terminology misleading? We have already or soon will have 1,600 American military personnel back to Iraq. And I say ''back.'' I know that you emphasized earlier in your statement, we didn't want to rehash old things, but I think it would be remiss in saying if we didn't say that ISIL wouldn't have been as successful as it has that thus far in taking land and literally slaughtering so many people had the U.S. not pulled the troops out.

When I have been to Iraq, every time that I was there, I think, everybody, our military personnel, the Iraqis, our diplomats, everybody anticipated that there would be a residual U.S. force there. And you talk about snatching defeat from the jaws of victory, I think that is exactly what happened here. But I digress.

Back to the 1,600 U.S. military personnel and probably more that will be on the ground there. And I know that is for training and it is for intelligence purposes and it is for targeting our air power and so forth.

But my question is: Is the administration really being straight with the American people when you keep emphasizing no boots on the ground? And isn't this 1,600 military personnel, at the present time, likely to go up and perhaps significantly?

Secretary KERRY. Well, you raise two important things, and I would like to speak both of them quickly. And I will answer your question.

The Islamic State, they call themselves obviously what they want to call themselves. We shouldn't compound the sin by allowing them to get away with it and calling them what they are not. They are not a state, and they do not represent Islam. And as I said earlier, now religious leaders, Islamic leaders are reclaiming legitimate Islam; and they are separating it, too. So I wouldn't compound the crime by calling them a state whatsoever.

They are the enemy of Islam. That is what they are. And as the 21 clerics yesterday said in Saudi Arabia, they are, in fact, the order of Satan. And there is nothing in Islam that condones or suggests people should go out and rape women and sell off young girls or give them as gifts to jihadists and, you know, cut people's heads off and tie people's hands behind their backs and put them on their knees and shoot them in the head. These are war crimes, and they are crimes against humanity. And we need to make clear that that is exactly what is the reality here.

Mr. CHABOT. And not to interrupt you, Mr. Secretary.

Secretary KERRY. Yeah.

Mr. CHABOT. And I agree with all the things you have said as far as the things they have done are horrific. No question about that. But it is clear to me that their motivation is their religious fervor, this fanaticism, however misguided it is. I mean, that is their motivation.

Secretary KERRY. Well, I don't know. They use that. I don't know if that is in truth. It is part of it. The caliphate is certainly on the minds of many. But I think a lot of them are thugs and criminals and people who simply want to go out and maraud and vanquish and be opposed to modernity and a whole bunch of other things here.

Mr. CHABOT. I certainly agree with you there.

Secretary KERRY. There is a lot of stuff going on there. With respect to troops and the President, the President has again and again said no combat troops. He just said it yesterday at CENTCOM very, very clearly.

I think I have his statement somewhere—here is what he said: ''Will not have a combat—the troops that have deployed to Iraq do not and will not have a combat mission.''

He has been absolutely up front about what they are going to be doing. They are going to be training and assisting, helping with intel, helping to build the capacity; but they will not have a combat role.

And what is important with respect to what you said about the expectation of troops staying in Iraq, yes, there was an expectation;

but we couldn't get the immunities and legal protection for them over the long term required for up to 10,000 troops. And, therefore, they didn't stay. But no one makes the judgment that what happened in Mosul happened because noncombat troops weren't there. These guys weren't going to be combat troops.

Chairman ROYCE. We are going to——

Secretary KERRY. What happened in Mosul happened because the troops there had no stake in fighting for Mosul, and the officers abandoned their posts. They had a greater allegiance to one person or to one sect than they did to Iraq and that is the problem.

Chairman ROYCE. We are going to go to Mr. Sires from New Jersey, ranking member of the Subcommittee on the Western Hemisphere.

Mr. SIRES. Thank you, Mr. Chairman.

Secretary KERRY. Can I just say to the committee, I have just been given a note that says that President Hollande has announced that he has authorized for France to provide air strikes in Iraq in response to a request from the Government of Iraq. And we obviously welcome that public announcement. That is one of the countries that we have been counting in our list.

Chairman ROYCE. Here here.

Mr. Sires.

Mr. SIRES. Thank you.

Mr. Secretary, thank you very much. I want to get back a little bit to the questions of the Kurds and see if we can get a little more detail. They have been playing such a strong role and such strong supporters of us. They have been basically holding the line, I guess, the Islamic State and providing Christians and other minorities with some safe haven.

But yesterday we had dinner with one of the ministers, and one of his biggest complaints was that they don't seem to be working with the new Government of Baghdad. And the other one was that the arms that we are providing, it comes in in trickles; and they need the arms necessary to continue the push.

Obviously, they have been our friends for many years. Obviously, we work with them. They have been loyal. I am just wondering if— I know it is going to take time, and I know you have a hard job putting all these groups together. But it would seem to me that this would be one of our priorities, to make sure that they have what they need to keep pushing ISIL back.

So I was just wondering, can you talk a little bit about that?

Secretary KERRY. I am delighted to talk a little bit about that. Look, I traveled to Erbil a few weeks ago, I think it was a few weeks ago, to meet with President Barzani and talk about the government formation and, also, about the steps that we would take.

So let me make it clear that first of all, we conducted targeted air strikes to stop ISIL's advance on Erbil. The Kurds were courageous, but I will tell you ISIL was advancing rapidly and President Obama made the emergency decision and we went in and we stopped them advancing.

Number 2, we immediately opened a joint operation center in Erbil to share information and intelligence at an unprecedented level.

Number 3, we led an international effort to provide the Peshmerga with weapons and ammunition. And, at least, 39 international flights have arrived in Erbil carrying arms for the KRG.

The coalition, up to now, has provided 22 million rounds of ammunition, tens of thousands of small arms, heavy mortars, heavy crew-served machine guns, anti-aircraft, anti-vehicle machine guns, and RPGs.

We have coordinated donors, like, Albania and Croatia with air transport providers, including U.K., Canada, Denmark, and Australia. And the President of the United States provided $25 million in drawdown funds to support operations which directly supported the KRG's supply efforts.

So I have to tell you, you know, I think some 17 flights of ours have gone in with these weapons and these arms. So we will continue. We are moving as fast as we can. And we are doing, I think, a pretty darn good job of getting weapons into the Kurds whom we have great respect for, the Peshmerga are a key component of this.

Now, I am concerned about what you said about how they have a sense of not working closely enough with the government.

Mr. SIRES. Well, one of the reasons they said that is because they are not even getting paid.

Secretary KERRY. Well, the government has just gotten going.

One of the parts of the agreement of the government formation was that an immediate $1 billion would be paid, and it was, as the government came together. There is up to $4 billion that is needed in order to pay back salaries. The next $1 billion is on its way. So I think that will be addressed because everybody understood that was part of the deal of the government coming together.

Mr. SIRES. Well, I think one of the concerns that they have is that we make these deals and then the Government of Baghdad does not keep up their end.

Secretary KERRY. Let me tell you, if the Government of Baghdad does not keep up their end—and we have made this crystal clear to them—they are going to have trouble seeing the United States of America do the things they need to do.

Mr. SIRES. Okay. Thank you very much.

Chairman ROYCE. Joe Wilson of South Carolina.

Mr. WILSON. Thank you, Mr. Chairman.

And thank you, Mr. Secretary, for being here.

Over the weekend, the President promised that, as we defeat ISIL, there will be no more mistakes. I look forward to working with you to avoid his mistake. The Obama mistake of underestimating ISIL as JV (junior varsity). Just 16 months ago, the President announced that the terrorist threat was being diminished; but at the same time, Dr. Fred Kagan of the American Enterprise Institute warned that they were growing safe havens of terrorists across North Africa, across the Middle East, and Central Asia.

The Obama mistake of failing to secure a basic security agreement with Iraq, this undermines the achievements of the American allies forces in promoting freedom in Iraq. And I particularly identified two of my sons served in Iraq. And I am very grateful for their service.

The Obama mistake of defense sequestration, downsizing the military as jihadists threats expand, allowing safe havens to attack American families worldwide.

The Obama mistake of failing to support the students of Iran's green revolution. We should remember the Iranian revolution supporters in Tehran carried signs very clearly in English; and they state, ''Death to Israel. Death to America.''

The Obama mistake of declaring a red line in Syria on chemical weapons and then blaming others. Clearly, the red line was stated first in a speech by the President on August 20, 2012.

The Obama mistake of releasing five murderous Taliban while negotiating with the terrorists. One of the terrorists was praised by the Taliban murders as the equivalent of 10,000 warriors to destroy America. The detention facility at Guantanamo Bay is more important than ever.

The Obama mistake of announcing an Afghan withdrawal date, disregarding conditions, putting Afghanistan and Pakistan at risk.

The Obama mistake of equating Hamas rocket attacks with Israel's self-defense. We should recognize Hamas' creed, ''We value death more than you value life.''

The Obama mistake of the Benghazi assassinations coverup. The Obama mistake of the Fort Hood massacre dismissed as workplace violence, and the Little Rock murderer as a drive-by shooting.

The President obviously needs to change course and adopt peace through strength. We know weakness endangers American families worldwide.

I believe the President should take action, remembering September 11th in the global war on terrorism.

And I am pleased to hear and I join with Congressman Sires in regard to our concern for the Kurdish region. The Kurdish region has been loyal allies of America for decades. The people are very brave and capable; but I have heard, as he, that the necessary military supplies are not being delivered. They are putting the Kurdish people at great risk. And so, again, what steps are being made to certainly guarantee and make sure that the Kurdish region receives the necessary supplies to defend themselves?

Secretary KERRY. I don't know where to begin, Congressman.

I will tell you where I will begin: And thank you for your two sons. We really appreciate their enormous contribution to the country.

And I obviously disagree with your judgment about mistakes, the red lines. We can have an argument about that, but I don't think it serves any great purpose here today.

So what I will do is, we can answer you on the record on that. But I do say thank you for your sons' service. That is what makes America great.

Mr. WILSON. And a restatement again of support for the Kurdish region and a commitment that we are going to follow through with weapons.

Secretary KERRY. Well, as I said, we are deeply committed. The Kurds are essential partners in this. We have enormous respect for the courage they have already shown and the fight they have already taken to ISIL. And we are aiming for success, Congressman. Believe me, the President is deeply committed to this effort.

The one thing I would say, after the list of mistakes, is, I honestly can't think of a President who has taken more risks and put more on the line to fight the continued struggle against terrorism, specifically, his efforts in Afghanistan, his efforts in Pakistan, his efforts in Yemen, his efforts in Mali, his efforts in Libya, I mean, you can run the list.

Mr. WILSON. And, Mr. Secretary, one final question. Yes or no, is America at war?

Secretary KERRY. Well, you know, I am going to answer that, Mr. Chairman. A lot of people are debating this idea of what do you call it. Do you call it war or don't you call it war?

It is not a war like Iraq where we invaded and had hundreds of thousands of troops mobilized and 16,000 sorties and so forth. It is not that kind of war.

But if you care about what you call it, it is a war similar to what we did with al-Qaeda and terror. And, sure, what I care about is not what we call it. I care about what we do, and I care about making sure we defeat ISIL.

And if you are more comfortable calling it a war against this enemy of Islam, then, please do so. We are happy. We would call it that. And it is much more important to focus on how we are going to do it.

Mr. WILSON. And action—you are correct.

Chairman ROYCE. The time has expired.

We are going to have to go to Gerry Connolly of Virginia.

Mr. CONNOLLY. You could say that with some enthusiasm, Mr. Chairman.

I was listening carefully to my colleague from South Carolina, and I must respectfully take issue. What happened in Syria last year was a signal failure by this Congress. In a very rare event, a President of the United States came to Congress and said, "Here is the problem, here is what I want to do about it, give me an authorization."

And what did we do? We dithered, we kvetched, we wrung our hands, we found all kinds of rationalizations for why we just couldn't bring ourselves to do it. And I think we damaged the United States' foreign policy, United States' standing, and our respectability as an institution. So if we are going to start finger pointing, let's start with ourselves.

Having said that, Mr. Secretary, welcome back to Congress.

Secretary KERRY. I was——

Mr. CONNOLLY. The fun never stops around here.

Mr. Secretary, you bravely served your country. You won medals for your service in an undeclared war in Southeast Asia. And at that time we had two Presidents who used the Gulf of Tonkin resolution basically to engage in a massive ground war in mainland Asia. That was a fairly flimsy basis upon which to wage war, and all of us of that generation are cognizant of that.

So I want to return—and I understand you are wearing a different hat today than you did when you were on the Senate Foreign Relations Committee. But we heard you say and we heard the President say, you welcome a congressional authorization. But, I guess, I would gently prod you. Don't you need it? Isn't it just as flimsy to cite a resolution for a different time, a different environment, a different challenge 13 years ago? And wouldn't it be better for our country, our allies, and for the mission we are undertaking to have a full-blown debate and to request that authorization as, I believe, the Constitution of the United States requires, but I know we are not going to agree. I want to give you an opportunity?

Secretary KERRY. Well, thank you, Congressman. Thank you for your original comment.

I think I said to you that, of course, it would be better to have an update. It would be better to have the Congress ratify and join in. It would be better to have the American people represented by the Congress through a good debate and what is happening, for sure. I haven't changed in all these years with respect to that.

But it is not necessary for the President to begin the process that he is beginning.

Mr. CONNOLLY. Mr. Secretary, if I can interrupt, because we have limited time. And you said you think you have all the authorization you need from that resolution of 13 years ago, the authorization?

Secretary KERRY. We are convinced. We have tested this very carefully with the lawyers and I have as good a set of lawyers as anywhere in the country and in the State Department and in the White House and they conclude, without any question, that ISIL began as al-Qaeda in Iraq. And the authorization clearly in 2005, 2006, 2007, 2008 referred to al-Qaeda in Iraq. Just standing up in 2013 a year ago and saying, "Hey, we are no longer going to be part of this because we happen to be worse than them and they don't like us anymore" doesn't get you out from under who you are and what you are trying to do and how you do it.

And, therefore, yes, it is a span of years. It wasn't something that any of us foresaw. But it doesn't affect the legality of the fact that this still is the same group that was doing what they did in Iraq. They called itself al-Qaeda in Iraq, they were part of al-Qaeda in Iraq, and now they are continuing to do the same in both places, in Iraq and in Syria.

We are convinced that the longstanding relationship they had with Bin Laden, the longstanding relationship with al-Qaeda, the continued desire to attack the United States and U.S. Persons, two of whom they have already murdered, we have the authority without any question; and it referred to the affiliates by the way. The language of the resolution referred to al-Qaeda and its affiliates. There is no question that these guys were an affiliate or are an affiliate.

So we are convinced we have it. But, yes, we are definitely stronger as a country, which is why the President came to Congress for the Syria authorization previously.

Mr. CONNOLLY. I thank you.

Chairman ROYCE. To Mr. Mike McCaul of Texas, chairman of the Committee on Homeland Security.

Mr. MCCAUL. Thank you, Mr. Chairman.

Thank you, Mr. Secretary, for being here today. We have known about this threat for well over a year. It has been festering.

I believe when the beheadings of the American journalists took place, it was a real wake-up call for the American people about the evil of ISIS or ISIL.

Then we watched, I think, the President go through what I perceived a very tortured decision-making process, I think, in part, because it defies his narrative that he campaigned on that he was going to end these wars. And it defies his legacy as well.

Having said that, I am glad that he finally came around on the issue, listened to General Dempsey, the chairman of the joint chiefs, that basically told him that we cannot defeat ISIS unless we go into Syria.

We just heard today, and I had a briefing on the Australian plot that was thwarted, this is an external operation, coming out of Syria, involving the beheadings of Australians and then a potential attack on their FBI.

As the chairman of Homeland Security, I don't want to see that happen in the United States; and I know nobody sitting here today wants to see that either. I would commend your pick of General Allen. I think that is probably one of the best decisions I have seen made.

I also think and I have always said that the moderate Muslims' most effective weapon we have against the extremist radical Muslim. That appears to be the strategy here with the vetting process.

Now, I have had my issues with the Syrian rebels in terms of throwing money and weapons without a proper vetting and training. I met with the Pentagon and was persuaded by the fact this is off-site in Saudi; that we do have the databases sufficient to properly train and vet them.

But eventually what turned me around was the fact that we are going to train the moderate Sunni Muslim to combat the extreme Sunni Muslim, and it is their fight. And we can provide assistance and capabilities and air strikes, and we will have advisors, and we will probably have special forces. But at the end of the day, it is their backyard.

And so my question to you is: When you met with these nations that, quite honestly, threw a lot of money indiscriminately that created this problem, it seems to me they ought to be fixing it as well.

What are they willing to put on the table to assist this effort? And, specifically, are they willing to put a ground force? Because that is what is lacking in Syria. We have that in Iraq, but we don't have that in Syria.

I am concerned that the number of 5,000, over a period of 6 months, when you are looking at 30,000 ISIS forces and growing every day, whether that is going to be a realistic, achievable strategy without more assistance from these other Nations and, particularly, the Arab world that, I think, has some responsibility to bear the burden.

Secretary KERRY. Well, Congressman, first of all, thank you for your leadership on Homeland Security and your service in there because that is key to our safety, obviously. And we appreciate that.

I think it is unfair to confuse careful with ''tortured.'' I have watched the President ask a lot of tough questions that are appropriate and look for consequences that need to be analyzed prior to making a Presidential decision. And I think careful is what people want in a President.

Secondly, the President has accepted General Dempsey's advice that you have to go into Syria, that you have to be able to impact

Syria; and he said that to the Nation. And I advocate the same thing. I think you cannot attack ISIL only in Iraq. You just can't do it.

If they go seek refuge in Syria and they have a safe haven there, that is directly contrary to the very policy we have pursued about not allowing sanctuary for al-Qaeda in Pakistan or elsewhere. So, you know, you can't contain. There is no containment with this group. There is no such thing as negotiation. There is nothing to negotiate. And I think everybody here understands that.

So that requires a willingness to go get the job done. Now, in that context, you are absolutely correct that money came from places that it shouldn't have come to some of these groups and they morphed. And I think people would sit there in a moment of candor and tell you today that they acknowledge that. But that is part of what is giving us the unity of purpose to rectify that now. So I am very hopeful.

You say ISIL is growing every day and there are only 5,000 opposition fighters. You go get the classified numbers. But the classified numbers say to us there are tens of thousands of opposition fighters today. Not 5,000. Five thousand is what the initial training can produce. And if we are successful, if, you know, this enemy of Islam can get set back sufficiently, young people and possible recruits are going to have a different attitude about where they might want to be and with whom. And that could change very rapidly.

So the numbers are something that could be in flux. I am not going to sit here and tell you with certainly it is only 5,000. That is the target. But I can tell you that I don't think these guys are 10 feet tall. And the intelligence tells us that, as we have begun to hit them, we have been able to prove that to some degree.

Chairman ROYCE. We go now to Mr. Ted Deutch of Florida, ranking member on the Subcommittee on Middle East and North Africa.

Mr. DEUTCH. Thank you, Mr. Chairman.

Thanks to you and the ranking member for ensuring this committee has an opportunity to discuss directly with the administration the U.S. strategy to the ISIL threat.

Mr. Secretary, thank you for being here today. Before going into my questions about this topic, I want to join Mr. Smith in thanking you for your statements about the Americans who have been held in Iran.

And, in particular, I would note that, as we approach the November deadline for nuclear talks with Iran, we will also be approaching yet another Thanksgiving that Bob Levinson will not be with his family. While I appreciate all of your efforts, I nevertheless want to continue to urge you to press the Iranians, as I know you do at every meeting, for any information on Mr. Levinson and urge them to show some humanity and some good faith by permitting Mr. Levinson to be reunited with his family.

The administration has outlined a comprehensive strategy for combating the ISIL terrorist threat that encompasses, not just a targeted air campaign, but efforts to cut off ISIL's financial support, strengthen moderate forces in the ground in Syria.

Mr. Secretary, you personally traveled to nearly every Arab state, securing the support of our partners in the region. You and the President have helped to build a strong international coalition, and I support your efforts. I commend you for them and I think we are grateful for them.

I just wanted to follow up on Mr. Connolly's questioning with a couple of points. One, I would like to associate myself with his comments about the actions of this Congress a year ago. But I would also like to just to suggest that while yesterday's vote was about authorizing funding to support the Syrian opposition, we do need to have a broader debate about authorizing the use of military force. That is not what yesterday's vote was.

And while you may be precisely right that the AUMF from 2001 legally gives you the authority that is necessary, that there are an awful lot of us who weren't here to participate in that debate and who would like the opportunity, on behalf of our constituents, to engage in a debate about the type of force that should be used, can be used and, in fact, then ultimately, once that determination is made, to authorize it on behalf of Americans today for this purpose. So I hope that we have that opportunity and I think that is something that the administration should want and should request.

Just shifting topics for a second. You were quoted in the press this week as saying that we are leaving channels of communication open with Iran. And I would like you to explain what exactly we are communicating to Iran, how much we know about Iran's support for the Shiite militias, whether Iranian forces are on the ground in Iraq and, finally, we are reminded that Iran continues to be the largest state sponsor of terrorism in the world; and that Iran with a nuclear weapon would not only empower its terrorist allies, like the Assad regime and Hezbollah, but it would spark an arm's race throughout the region that would be so damaging as extremist groups are marching throughout the Middle East.

So given that there is less than 2 months from the November 24th deadline for nuclear negotiations, if you could provide us with necessary assurances that our shared goal of destroying ISIL won't be used by Iran as a pretense for extending negotiations or for pressing the administration and our partners in those negotiations to accept anything less than an Iran that does not pose a threat in the region and to the world.

Secretary KERRY. Let me state unequivocally, there is no connection, relationship, dependency between what we are currently about to be engaged in with respect to this, you know, so called ISIL and these talks. And there is a real discipline on both sides with respect to the focus on the talks.

Now, everybody knows because we announced on the margins of the P5+1 talks that there was some inquiry about ISIL and the position of Iran and so forth. Iran is very opposed to ISIL, and it would be illogical, it would be almost diplomatic malpractice not to inquire, what their attitude is or what their attitude is about our engagement or whatever. That doesn't mean we are cooperating. We are not cooperating. There is no joint effort, but I think it is important. Diplomacy is communication, and mistakes are avoided by communicating.

So there is no coordination, there is no change in our attitude, there is no shift in policy, there is no linkage. But, yes, there has been and we are open to anything that could help to solve this problem, we will listen to——

Chairman ROYCE. Judge Ted Poe——

Secretary KERRY [continuing]. Without compromising our values and our interests.

Chairman ROYCE. We go to Judge Ted Poe of Texas, chairman of the Subcommittee on Terrorism, Nonproliferation, and Trade.

Mr. POE. Thank you, Mr. Secretary, for being here.

The United States has made a commitment to protect ethnic and religious minorities who have been subject to ISIS in Iraq. The unarmed residents of Camp Liberty have been attacked, as you know, seven times, resulting in the murder of 100 residents, wounding 1,000 others.

Myself and 26 other Members of Congress have sent you a letter, asking you specifically what now will be done to protect those members of Camp Liberty. I would like for you to respond to the letter in writing as opposed to this hearing today.

So I would like to move on to specifically what we are talking about with ISIS. The way I understand it, the United States' plan is to arm the people in Syria that have been vetted with the intent of, I suspect, defeating ISIS in Syria and, also, a strategy to defeat ISIS in Iraq at the same time.

I'm concerned about that, because we armed the rebels or the opposition in Libya; and now that hasn't turned out so well. Libya, to me, is a failed state. I have a series of questions.

You have made it clear that this is not Islamic philosophy. Tell me and the American people exactly who we are at war with. What would you call—I call them ISIS, Islamic State of Iraq and Syria.

What would you tell the American people? Okay, we are doing this support, we are at war, we are counterterrorism operation, whatever you want to call it. Who is the enemy? Define the enemy for me. What would you call them?

Secretary KERRY. Well, Congressman, let me say very quickly, I share your concern. The administration shares your concern about the Mujahedin-e Khalq who have been too long in Camp Liberty, and we recognize that. We have been able to work to get 384 residents out of there.

Mr. POE. Excuse me, Mr. Secretary. I would like you to respond to that question in writing because of the time limit.

Secretary KERRY. Okay. Fine.

Mr. POE. You just go ahead and answer the question: Who are we at war with? I call them ISIS. Who would you call these?

Secretary KERRY. Well, I call them the enemy of Islam, because that is what, I think, they are. And they certainly don't represent a state, even though they try to claim to.

Mr. POE. So officially we should refer to them as the enemy of Islam.

Secretary KERRY. Well, I do.

Mr. POE. Okay.

Secretary KERRY. I don't know if there is an official whatever.

Mr. POE. Well, why don't we tell the American people——

Secretary KERRY. I hope you join me in doing that, because that is what I think they are; and I don't think they deserve to have a reference in their name that gives them legitimacy.

Mr. POE. Are they the enemy of the United States?

Secretary KERRY. Beg your pardon?

Mr. POE. Are they the enemy of the United States?

Secretary KERRY. They are an enemy of humanity.

Mr. POE. So they are an enemy of the U.S., too?

Secretary KERRY. Among others.

Mr. POE. Okay.

Secretary KERRY. Among many others——

Mr. POE. Well, I am just looking specifically at the national security interest of the United States.

Secretary KERRY. Definitively, it is in the national security interest of our country, with Americans over there with passports, learning how to fight and taking part in this——

Mr. POE. And I agree with you, they shouldn't come back unless they are in handcuffs. I agree with that.

Secretary KERRY. For all those reasons, yes.

Mr. POE. What is the long-term strategy? Is it to defeat this group, ISIS, if you don't mind me calling them that?

Secretary KERRY. Yes. Yes, it is. You know, this is my best entreaty to call them something but that is all right.

Mr. POE. All right. But that is the long-term goal of the United States——

Secretary KERRY. The long-term goal is to end their capacity to engage in acts of terror and terrorize to be a threat to the United States and others and to destabilize the region.

Mr. POE. Do you suspect that this—as long as it takes, is that really the position of the United States? However long it takes, we are going to defeat this group?

Secretary KERRY. Well, the answer is, if your goal is to defeat them, you better be prepared to do it however long it takes. But that doesn't mean it is going to have to take forever. And I think if we put together the right coalition, if we all join together and support the right strategy and do the right things and follow through, I am confident that we can defeat ISIL.

Mr. POE. By any means necessary we are going to defeat them, or are we just going to defeat them with certain strategies——

Secretary KERRY. Well, we have a strategy, and we think it can work. And we have other options within that strategy, if the first steps don't.

Mr. POE. But if the Syrian rebels aren't successful in defeating them on their own, we have contingency plans to follow up?

Secretary KERRY. There are other options. We are not making those plans right now because we plan to defeat them the way we are going.

Chairman ROYCE. We are going to go to Mr. Brian Higgins of New York.

Mr. HIGGINS. Thank you, Mr. Chairman.

Mr. Secretary, thank you for your extraordinary work on behalf of America.

You had indicated you characterize the Free Syrian Army as secular and moderate at the beginning of your statement. And although that certainly characterizes it as part of the story, I think there is a lot more to tell with respect to this organization.

It is between 40,000 and 50,000 fighters. Their worst fighters, by most accounts, are those that secular and moderate. Their best fighters are Islamic extremists and al-Qaeda affiliates. They are not unified. They lack an effective command structure. They have no political center.

And the problem is, when you have 1,000 militias and no political center, there are only sides to pick. So I would have some concerns about our reliance on the Free Syrian Army to provide the ground troops strength to help us succeed in this mission.

Obviously, we can't depend on the Iraqi army. The United States spent $25 billion to train and build a new army. The troop strength of the Iraqi army was estimated to be 250,000. And when ISIS moved on them, they ran.

So my question is: You know, the Kurdish military up in Kurdistan, the Peshmerga, is estimated to be anywhere between 80 and 190,000 fighters. They are regarded as pro-American. They are well equipped and well trained and experienced. They are reliable allies, as they assisted us in apprehending a Bin Laden ally in 2003. There is a stable political situation in Kurdistan. They recognize minority rights.

Are we partnering with the right organization in that part of the world to achieve our objectives? And why wouldn't we try to engage, to a greater degree, the Peshmerga, given their history of reliance? So I would ask you that question.

Secretary KERRY. Well, let me begin. A very good question, Congressman. I just begin by saying to you that the numbers that you put out with respect to the size of the opposition, we don't agree that those are the limit of the numbers, particularly when you include the more Islamic of those fighters and, particularly, when you include some of the bad guys in that grouping. We don't include those.

When I tell you there are tens of thousands, I am not including al-Nusra and people that we are not going to have anything to do with and that we don't agree with, obviously. So our numbers are a little bit different from where you begin.

Secondly, we are not relying, obviously, exclusively, on them. We are working with the Kurds. That is why you saw such a massive amount of support going into the Kurds, with the permission of the Government of Baghdad; and that is why they sort of bypassed and we went directly to them with their permission.

So I think you need to recognize what is already happening. The Kurds indeed can be a critical partner in this effort.

Mr. HIGGINS. Yield back.

Chairman ROYCE. We go now to Matt Salmon of Arizona.

Mr. SALMON. Thank you, Mr. Secretary, for coming to speak to this committee about this administration's plan to defeat ISIS.

I do believe that it is unfortunate you couldn't come and answer our questions in advance of the House voting on the very issue; but I am pleased that, at least, we could get some of these questions answered today.

My first question is: Just 5 weeks ago, the President said it was a fantasy that the Free Syrian Army could take up arms and lead the fight. Now, they are a cornerstone of our strategy to defeat ISIS.

What has changed to make the Free Syrian Army now a credible partner where before the President considered them a punch line?

Secretary KERRY. Well, what the President said, actually, that comment was made way back when. It came out recently; he was referring, when he made the comment, which was made way back when, he was referring back to the time originally when, in the last administration, people were talking in the very beginning about whether or not they should be armed and so forth. And he, as you know, had reservations about that at that time. And the reason is that, at that time, there was not the sense of structure and capacity and definition that there is today.

So there has been a long road between what the President actually applied those comments to and what we are looking at today. We now have tens of thousands of people who are, by the way, the principal bulwark against ISIL in Syria today. They are the ones who drove them out of Idlib province. They are the ones who are taking them on in the Damascus suburbs. They are the ones who are fighting in Aleppo.

So what has happened is, over time, a lot of people came to this fight, a lot of people gained experience. Some went off and joined the most radical groups, and you know, we are not working with them. But a lot of them chose to be part of the Free Syrian Army and to stay away from the more extreme and violent strain.

So, yeah, it is complicated. There are divisions. You have to understand, the principal behind all these people coming to Syria is Assad. Assad is the magnet that is drawing all of these foreign fighters there.

Mr. SALMON. And he is their top priority. I understand that.

I just have one other question, and I am going to finish early and let somebody have a chance. But there have been allegations that the so-called moderates over in the region are the ones that sold our reporters to ISIL to have their heads cut off. Is there any intelligence that supports that?

Secretary KERRY. Actually, there is intelligence that refutes it. That is an ISIL disinformation claim. And in fact, that never happened. It is, as I said, it is false information that was put out by ISIL itself.

Mr. SALMON. Thank you.

I will yield back.

Chairman ROYCE. Thank you.

We will go to Karen Bass of California, ranking member of the Africa Subcommittee.

Ms. BASS. Thank you, Mr. Chairman.

Like my colleague, Representative Meeks, I also took a very difficult vote last night and voted for the amendment because I didn't see another alternative.

Some people that are unhappy with my vote believe that there is another approach and another strategy other than air strikes and arming the rebels. So I thought I would ask you two quick questions. Why isn't there a diplomatic or a political approach or strategy to address ISIL? And then what are the lessons learned from the NATO intervention in Libya? And how are the lessons being applied to today?

Thank you.

Secretary KERRY. Well, first of all, the United States of America has a firm policy, which I believe is the right policy, that we don't negotiate with terrorists. And I can't think of a group that is more defining of modern day terrorism than this group.

Secondly, there is nothing that they want that you can negotiate about. They have decreed a caliphate, their life philosophy and pursuit at this moment is marauding, buying young women, selling them, raping people, killing them. Anybody who isn't them, you can be killed. They are avowed genocidists, and they went after whole groups of people defined only by not being them.

If you were Yazidi, you would get killed; Shia, you would get killed; if you are Christian, you get killed. And they have made it clear. There is nothing to negotiate about, either you join Islam or you die. What is the negotiation?

So that is pretty straightforward stuff.

Ms. BASS. And the other question about the lessons learned from NATO intervention in Libya and how——

Secretary KERRY. Well the lesson learned from NATO was it was absolutely the right—the President made the right decision to intervene because of what was going to happen in Benghazi. Regrettably, and the President would be the first to tell you this, in all countries that we are engaged and by the way, you know, certain countries had taken the lead on that, as you know, with respect to kinetic activity.

We agreed to support and be supportive. And certain folks were tasked with the follow-up afterwards. The President would be the first to tell you that all Nations were insufficiently focused on the follow-up.

And that is the biggest lesson of all. You cannot leave a vacuum. You have got to come in with sufficient capacity. And I don't think there was sufficient follow-up in Libya. And everybody would say that.

Ms. BASS. Mr. Chairman, I yield my time.

Chairman ROYCE. Okay. Well, we want to thank the Secretary for his time today.

We have covered a lot of ground about the ISIL threat, both in terms of security and in terms of their threat to humanity. We are going to cover more in the weeks to come. And we will also want to continue to be in touch on other important issues in Iraq.

Mr. Secretary, like the safety of those at Camp Ashraf. Many have lost their lives. We want to make certain as we continue this dialogue that the State Department takes concerted steps here in order to protect their security.

For now we stand adjourned. I thank the members. The vote is on on the House floor.

Secretary KERRY. Thank you very much, Mr. Chairman.

Chairman ROYCE. Thank you, Mr. Secretary.

[Whereupon, at 1:33 p.m., the committee was adjourned.]

APPENDIX

FULL COMMITTEE HEARING NOTICE
COMMITTEE ON FOREIGN AFFAIRS
U.S. HOUSE OF REPRESENTATIVES
WASHINGTON, DC 20515-6128

Edward R. Royce (R-CA), Chairman

September 11, 2014

TO: MEMBERS OF THE COMMITTEE ON FOREIGN AFFAIRS

You are respectfully requested to attend an OPEN hearing of the Committee on Foreign Affairs, to be held in Room 2172 of the Rayburn House Office Building (and available live on the Committee website at http://www.ForeignAffairs.house.gov):

DATE: Thursday, September 18, 2014

TIME: 11:30 a.m.

SUBJECT: The ISIS Threat: Weighing the Obama Administration's Response

WITNESS: The Honorable John F. Kerry
Secretary of State
U.S. Department of State

By Direction of the Chairman

The Committee on Foreign Affairs seeks to make its facilities accessible to persons with disabilities. If you are in need of special accommodations, please call 202/225-5021 at least four business days in advance of the event, whenever practicable. Questions with regard to special accommodations in general (including availability of Committee materials in alternative formats and assistive listening devices) may be directed to the Committee.

COMMITTEE ON FOREIGN AFFAIRS
MINUTES OF FULL COMMITTEE HEARING

Day __Thursday__ Date __09/18/14__ Room __2172__

Starting Time __11:34 a.m.__ Ending Time __1:33 p.m.__

Recesses __0__ (___to___)(___to___)(___to___)(___to___)(___to___)(___to___)

Presiding Member(s)

Edward R. Royce, Chairman

Check all of the following that apply:

Open Session ✓
Executive (closed) Session ☐
Televised ✓

Electronically Recorded (taped) ✓
Stenographic Record ✓

TITLE OF HEARING:

The ISIS Threat: Weighing the Obama Administration's Response

COMMITTEE MEMBERS PRESENT:

See Attendance Sheet.

NON-COMMITTEE MEMBERS PRESENT:

Rep. Sheila Jackson Lee

HEARING WITNESSES: Same as meeting notice attached? Yes ✓ No ☐
(If "no", please list below and include title, agency, department, or organization.)

STATEMENTS FOR THE RECORD: *(List any statements submitted for the record.)*

Rep. Eliot Engel
Rep. Gerald Connolly

TIME SCHEDULED TO RECONVENE _____
or
TIME ADJOURNED __1:33 p.m.__

Jean Marter, Director of Committee Operations

HOUSE COMMITTEE ON FOREIGN AFFAIRS
FULL COMMITTEE HEARING

PRESENT	MEMBER	PRESENT	MEMBER
X	Edward R. Royce, CA	X	Eliot L. Engel, NY
X	Christopher H. Smith, NJ	X	Eni F.H. Faleomavaega, AS
X	Ileana Ros-Lehtinen, FL	X	Brad Sherman, CA
X	Dana Rohrabacher, CA	X	Gregory W. Meeks, NY
X	Steve Chabot, OH	X	Albio Sires, NJ
X	Joe Wilson, SC	X	Gerald E. Connolly, VA
X	Michael T. McCaul, TX	X	Theodore E. Deutch, FL
X	Ted Poe, TX	X	Brian Higgins, NY
X	Matt Salmon, AZ	X	Karen Bass, CA
X	Tom Marino, PA	X	William Keating, MA
X	Jeff Duncan, SC	X	David Cicilline, RI
X	Adam Kinzinger, IL	X	Alan Grayson, FL
X	Mo Brooks, AL	X	Juan Vargas, CA
X	Tom Cotton, AR	X	Bradley S. Schneider, IL
	Paul Cook, CA	X	Joseph P. Kennedy III, MA
X	George Holding, NC	X	Ami Bera, CA
	Randy K. Weber, Sr., TX	X	Alan S. Lowenthal, CA
X	Scott Perry, PA		Grace Meng, NY
	Steve Stockman, TX	X	Lois Frankel, FL
X	Ron DeSantis, FL	X	Tulsi Gabbard, HI
X	Doug Collins, GA	X	Joaquin Castro, TX
X	Mark Meadows, NC		
X	Ted S. Yoho, FL		
X	Sean Duffy, WI		
X	Curt Clawson, FL		

47

47

MATERIAL SUBMITTED FOR THE RECORD BY THE HONORABLE ELIOT L. ENGEL, A
REPRESENTATIVE IN CONGRESS FROM THE STATE OF NEW YORK

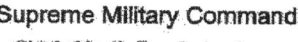

Supreme Military Command

Chief of Staff - Free Syrian Army

هيئة الأركان العامة للجيش السوري
الحر

صادر: 12
تاريخ: 17/09/2014

September 17, 2014

Statement to the Syrian people

As Chief of Staff of the Supreme Military Command, I hereby reaffirm the Free
Syrian Army's continued commitment to removing the twin terrorists Bashar al-
Assad and Abu Bakr al-Baghdadi from Syrian soil.

The heroes of the Free Syrian Army have sacrificed thousands of brave souls in
the fight against the impostor "Islamic State" over the past year. We fully plan to
continue this fight until Baghdadi's complete and utter defeat.

The Assad regime collaborates with "Islamic State" and other terrorist groups like
Hezbollah that seek our extermination. We will be unable to finish off "Islamic
State" without also acting to stop Assad's barbaric assaults.

We call upon the world community, and the United States Congress in particular,
to fulfill their humanitarian and security responsibilities by providing the Free
Syrian Army with robust support to bring a Syria free from terrorism in all its
forms.

Brigadier General Abdul Ilah Al-Bashir

Chief of Staff
Supreme Military Command
Free Syrian Army

Statement for the Record
Submitted by Mr. Connolly of Virginia

The terrorist group known as the Islamic State of Iraq and the Levant (ISIL) is, without question, a threat the United States must address. ISIL's program of genocide is undermining the stability of Iraq, threatening our partners in the Iraqi Kurdistan Region, and reversing gains made by moderate forces in Syria against the brutal dictator, Bashar al-Assad. With the rise of ISIL, we have witnessed humanitarian crises, the butchery of two American journalists, and the systematic elimination of an ancient Christian community that has coexisted with other religious communities for nearly two millennia. America cannot stand idly by as ISIL sets the region on fire and begins to export its brand of violent extremism.

The President has laid out a bold and decisive strategy to lead a multilateral operation designed to degrade and ultimately destroy ISIL.

Congress has a constructive and collaborative role to play in this effort. This committee has examined on several occasions the rise of ISIL and the destabilizing role it has played in the region. As our discussion turns to how the U.S. will respond to this insidious threat, Congress should seize this opportunity to assert its constitutional role and codify the parameters of our mission against ISIL. Almost one year ago, in response to the President's consultation with Congress on the deepening crisis in Syria, I introduced a resolution authorizing the President to carry out airstrikes against the Assad regime. In that case, Congress chose to demur.

In light of the ISIL threat, Congress must make clear for the public and our partners our firm resolve to take swift and decisive action. The Administration maintains that the President has the constitutional and statutory authority to carry out military operations against ISIL based in part on the 2001 Authorization for the Use of Military Force (AUMF). However, a new AUMF, specific to this operation, would guard against mission creep and would likely unite a broad coalition of stakeholders around the effort to eliminate ISIL. I believe the President would find bipartisan support in Congress for airstrikes in Iraq and Syria. This tactic has thus far effectively bolstered our partners on the ground, protected American assets, and facilitated humanitarian missions.

Yesterday, the House of Representatives passed an amendment to H. J. Res. 124, the continuing resolution, to authorize the President to train and equip appropriately vetted Syrian opposition forces. I appreciate that the measure addressed many concerns that were raised about this proposal. First, the amendment provided for careful Congressional oversight. The Department of Defense must report to Congress on the vetting process for trainees 15 days prior to providing any such assistance. The President must report to Congress on how this operation fits within our overall regional strategy. The Department of Defense must also submit a report every 90 days updating Congress on the status of the operation. These are prudent measures and consistent with the Constitutional role of Congressional oversight. Second, the amendment did not provide a blank check for military operations. No additional funds are provided by the measure, and the Department of Defense must submit reprogramming requests to Congress. Third, it did not allow for an open-ended commitment. The limited activities authorized by the amendment will remain in effect until the earlier of the date of the expiration of the CR or the enactment of the FY2015 National Defense Authorization Act.

I hope that our examination of the ISIL threat and the U.S. response can see beyond the days and weeks ahead. Such a consideration includes questions about Iraq's central government and its role going forward. Can we trust its leaders to abandon the sectarian strife that helped provide ISIL a foothold in Iraq? Are Iraqi military forces able to take up the charge the Kurdistan Peshmerga have faithfully served throughout this conflict, and will the central government demonstrate its willingness to act in good faith with domestic partners by releasing revenue owed to the Kurdistan Regional Government? In Syria, Bashar al-Assad remains in power and at odds with ISIL forces. Does arming the moderate opposition forces serve the dual purposes of fighting ISIL and bringing about the end of the Assad regime? More fundamentally, as our intelligence estimates of the number of ISIL fighters grow by the day, is the initiative even sufficient to meet our goal of defeating ISIL?

Thank you to Secretary of State Kerry for coming before the Committee today. I look forward to your testimony and hope that it cements a cooperative effort between Congress and the Administration to respond to the ISIL threat in order to protect the national security interests of the United States and its allies.

Questions for the Record
Submitted by the Honorable Alan Lowenthal
To Secretary John Kerry

Question 1:

Do we not need a new AUMF?

Answer:

The President is relying on the 2001 Authorization for Use of Military Force (AUMF) (Public Law 107-40) to conduct airstrikes against ISIL. In addition, the President has the statutory authority to conduct airstrikes against ISIL under the 2002 AUMF (Public Law 107-243) in at least some circumstances.

The President welcomes congressional support for military efforts to combat ISIL, and he would welcome enactment of a new, limited authorization for the use of military force that would specifically address the threat posed by ISIL and would repeal the 2002 AUMF. As the President has said, our democracy is strongest when the President and Congress act together on matters involving the use of U.S. military force.

Question 2:

Tell me what "vetting" means? Why do you believe it will keep weapons from falling into the "wrong" hands? Who will do the vetting?

Answer:

The Department of Defense, with the support of the entire interagency, is committed to counterterrorism and human rights vetting procedures with respect to efforts to train and equip Syria's moderate opposition. I refer you to the Department of Defense for any additional details.

Question 3:

Why do you believe there are "moderates" in Syria?

Answer:

The Syrian opposition includes a number of political and armed components. Elements of the moderate opposition have been fighting ISIL for many months and at times have clashed with al-Nusrah Front, another designated Foreign Terrorist Organization, even as they fight the Asad regime.

The main moderate political entity is the Syrian Opposition Coalition (SOC), which the United States and numerous other countries have recognized as the legitimate representative of the Syrian people. The SOC has 117 representatives and is led by President Hadi al-Bahra. The United States has been working with the SOC since early in the conflict. The SOC has stated that it is committed to a future Syria inclusive of all ethnic and religious groups. The SOC leadership welcomed President Obama's initiative and the train and equip program, reiterating its commitment to fight ISIL.

The SOC includes representatives of the armed moderate opposition, many of whom refer to themselves as the Free Syrian Army. The SOC, when possible, provides funding to moderate brigades in the field. The armed opposition was initially formed to defend local communities from regime attacks on civilians and peaceful protesters.